SOUTH DAKOTA'S MATHIS MURDERS

HORROR IN THE HEARTLAND

NOEL HAMIEL

In South Dakota's Mathis Murders, *Noel Hamiel employs the sharp eye of an old-fashioned newspaperman—drawing on decades of managing South Dakota newsrooms—and the research skills of a gumshoe reporter and spools out a story that rivals Truman Capote's In Cold Blood, only one set in South Dakota instead of Kansas. It is uneasy reading for those not used to dark tales encroaching on normally peaceful prairie places.*
—Jon K. Lauck, author, historian and founding president of the Midwestern History Association

Mystery is a key characteristic of police and legal work, and in South Dakota's Mathis Murders, *the author has revisited one of this state's most infamous criminal puzzles. Starting with the Mathis triple slaying in 1981 and continuing through the trial and years that follow, the book reveals why even today debate continues over the case's outcome and the reasons it may never be resolved. Rich in detail and dialogue, the book paints compelling pictures of some of the state's top prosecution and defense lawyers and how they sought tactical advantage inside the courtroom and out. After forty years, it is a story that needed to be told.*
—Marty Jackley, former attorney general and United States attorney for South Dakota

The Mathis murders remain one of the most tragic—and unresolved—crimes in South Dakota history. Before time erases all living memory of the case, Noel Hamiel has done us the public service of interviewing many of the people involved in the investigation and trial. He has spun those conversations and his thorough research into an authoritative and gripping narrative, employing all of the fairness, accuracy and clarity he honed during his decades as a South Dakota newsman.
—Seth Tupper, longtime South Dakota journalist, author and supervising senior producer for South Dakota Public Broadcasting

Noel Hamiel skillfully assembles all the details—and even reports some new ones—in this absorbing and well-written account of the horrific murders of a thirty-year-old farm wife, Ladonna Mathis, and her two young boys, Brian, age four, and Patrick, age two, in their rural South Dakota home. For those who know the story, and those who don't, this book will take you right back in time as Hamiel paints a picture of the scene of the crime, the ensuing investigation, and the month-long courtroom drama where husband and father John Mathis was found not guilty of the shooting deaths. A retired newspaper reporter and editor, Hamiel sprinkles new interviews and reflections throughout this thorough retelling of a tragedy that still finds its way into the headlines some forty years later.
—Kim Galliano, former reporter and editor of the *Daily Republic*, Mitchell, South Dakota

Published by The History Press
Charleston, SC
www.historypress.com

Copyright © 2022 by Noel Hamiel
All rights reserved

First published 2022

Manufactured in the United States

ISBN 9781540251824

Library of Congress Control Number: 2022930146

Notice: The information in this book is true and complete to the best of our knowledge. It is offered without guarantee on the part of the author or The History Press. The author and The History Press disclaim all liability in connection with the use of this book.

All rights reserved. No part of this book may be reproduced or transmitted in any form whatsoever without prior written permission from the publisher except in the case of brief quotations embodied in critical articles and reviews.

To the men and women of South Dakota law enforcement

CONTENTS

Acknowledgments	9
Introduction	11
1. A Call for Help	15
2. Investigation	20
3. Indictment	28
4. Who Was John Mathis?	35
5. A Battle of Titans	40
6. Trial Begins	47
7. Prosecution Presses Ahead	55
8. A Matter of Motive	63
9. Portrait of a Good Woman	70
10. Mathis Defense Pushes Back	74
11. Courtroom Eloquence	82
12. Jury Deliberates	88
13. Not Guilty, but Not Free	94
14. Unresolved	99
15. Reflections	107
Interviews	117
Notes	119
Index	125
About the Author	128

ACKNOWLEDGMENTS

Former Davison County sheriff Lyle Swenson and former deputy sheriff Doug Kirkus were of invaluable help in providing information. Although both were intimately involved in the investigation, they did not attempt to influence my research in any way.

Davison County sheriff Steve Brink did an important service in making available the investigation files from the case.

Tim Bormann, chief of staff for the South Dakota Attorney General's Office, was instrumental in providing access to the state Department of Criminal Investigation files.

Many others associated with the case granted interviews and for their help I'm eternally grateful. They are listed in the "Interviews" section and included as sources in the text of the book.

I also wish to thank the Archives Center of the State Historical Society for making their materials available.

A heartfelt thanks to Kim Galliano, a good friend and fine editor, whose suggestions made the original manuscript much better. I am also indebted to valued colleague Seth Tupper for his editorial help.

Finally, grateful thanks to my wife, Janet, for her patience and her role as the manuscript's first reader.

INTRODUCTION

The metal machine shed still stands where it did forty years ago, when it witnessed the murders of a thirty-year-old farm wife and two of her sons.

Asleep in their beds in the makeshift home because of a house fire, Ladonna Ann Mathis, Brian and Patrick didn't hear the killer approach them, wielding a .22-caliber rifle.

He pointed the gun at Ladonna's head and pulled the trigger. The bullet, fired from several inches away, entered near the left ear and, in the words of the forensic pathologist, caused the lethal wound. A second gunshot wound to the left side of the neck did not "appear to involve any vital structures."

The coroner's report did not say which wound occurred first.

Not so in the case of Patrick, age two. The killer's first bullet entered the back of the neck, passing through the soft tissue and exiting near the left eye. It did not kill him.

The second bullet tracked across the base of the skull and severed the spinal cord before exiting the body. It caused near-instantaneous death, but the coroner's report said it was impossible to estimate how much time may have elapsed between the first and second shots.

"Patrick was alive with a beating heart after he sustained an injury to his muscle," forensic pathologist Brad Randall said of the first shot.

A gruesome picture emerged from the court testimony: "At some point later," after the first shot, "[Patrick] either sat up or kneeled in bed. At that point he sustained the second wound," Dr. Randall testified.

Patrick was lying on his stomach when the first shot was fired, but his body was found on its back. Two separate pools of blood were also found in Patrick's bed.

Introduction

Brian, age four, died instantly from a gunshot wound to the head in front of the right ear, which severed his spinal cord.

The brutality of the killings shocked the state and sent reverberations through the small farming community of Mount Vernon, located nine miles southwest of the Mathis farm.

First disbelief, then shock and, finally, horror set in.

The Mathises appeared to be a typical farm family. Hardworking. Churchgoing. No known enemies.

What could possibly explain what would later be described as the most notorious murders in the state's history?

For all of its quiet, rural nature, South Dakota by the 1970s and '80s was experiencing some of the same problems confronting more populous parts of the country. The state had survived the Great Depression and the Dust Bowl, but those events had culled farm families unable to hang on and sent many of them west to California, where jobs were plentiful. South Dakota rebounded after World War II and remained primarily an agricultural state. When the murders occurred on September 8, 1981, South Dakota was no stranger to illegal drugs, which had been a concern to law enforcement since the 1960s. Some speculated that this growing problem was connected to the Mathis murders. Still, compared to most parts of the nation, South Dakota was tranquil, traditional and safe. Which is why the murders of three farm family members as they lay sleeping in their beds were, to many, simply incomprehensible.

Not that the state was immune to violence or killings. Murder came early to Dakota Territory, the most famous occurring in 1877 with the shooting of James Butler "Wild Bill Hickok." The shooter, Jack McCall, who was upset about losing money to Hickok a day earlier, sneaked up behind him in a Deadwood saloon and shot him in the back of the head. Initially found innocent by a miners' court shortly after the shooting, McCall was retried in Yankton and hanged on March 1, 1877.

The Mathis murders, while setting a new threshold for grisly horror, foreshadowed violence to come.

One of those violent acts was the 1987 stabbing death of three-year-old Abby Lynn at the hands of her mother, Debra Jenner, a Huron woman. Jenner was convicted of stabbing her daughter more than seventy times with a knife and a toy metal airplane. It was one of South Dakota's most horrific crimes.

In 1990, Donald Moeller kidnapped, raped and stabbed to death nine-year-old Becky O'Connell of Sioux Falls. Moeller was convicted and sentenced in 1992, but his appeals lasted more than twenty years, until he

Introduction

finally admitted in early October 2012 that he had killed the girl. He was executed by lethal injection on October 30, 2012.

Carl Swanson of Hosmer, South Dakota, shot his estranged wife and two of their children in May 1993. After fleeing with his infant son, he shot the boy and then himself. The one-year-old son later died.

In 1999, Robert Leroy Anderson of Sioux Falls was convicted of raping and murdering Piper Streyle, twenty-eight, and of kidnapping and murdering Larisa Dumansky, twenty-nine. Anderson was sentenced to death by lethal injection, but he committed suicide in his cell by hanging himself with a bedsheet on March 30, 2003.

On March 13, 2000, Elijah Page, Briley Piper and Darrell Hoadley were convicted of the torture and murder of Chester Allan Poage. Page and Piper were sentenced to death, and Hoadley was sentenced to life in prison. Page was executed by lethal injection on July 11, 2007. Piper remains on death row.

Eric Robert posed as a police officer, abducted an eighteen-year-old woman and forced her into the trunk of his car. In 2006, he was sentenced to eighty years in prison. In 2011, he and an accomplice beat to death corrections officer Ronald Johnson with a pipe. Robert was executed by lethal injection on October 15, 2012.

The stark difference between the Mathis murders and the others is that no one was convicted of killing Ladonna Mathis and her two sons.

To this day, the failure to arrest and convict the murderer haunts the principals in the case. The prosecutors have explanations for the acquittal of John Mathis and believe that the right person was arrested. Mathis has maintained that he wants the murderer apprehended, and for many years following the case, his family offered a reward for information leading to the arrest and conviction of the assailant.

Technically, the case remains open, though inactive. Some of the key figures, such as Judge Thomas Anderst, Attorney General Mark Meierhenry and defense counsel Rick Johnson, have died. But many others who were intimately involved in the case are speaking out, trying to explain what happened on that late summer morning and in the trial that followed.

What was the motive for the cold-blooded killing of a farm wife and two of her children? Why did John Mathis sustain only a minor wound? What happened to the murder weapon? Were there other suspects? What was going through the minds of the jurors?

If there is one thing that both sides likely could agree on, even today, it is that justice was not served.

Chapter 1

A CALL FOR HELP

When the phone rings in the wee hours of the morning, bad news often follows.

For Doug Kirkus, a six-year deputy sheriff, taking inconvenient calls was part of the job. His home phone and the Mount Vernon police number were listed as one. But this call—at 3:54 a.m.—was far different from anything Kirkus had ever experienced.

He rolled over and picked up the receiver. Stress colored the voice on the other end.

"Doug, this is John Mathis. Could you get out here right away? I need help, send an ambulance quick."

Now fully awake, Kirkus asked Mathis what had happened, and whether due to how the words were said or the horrendousness of the crime, it didn't register clearly.

"He wasn't hollering or talking real loud," Kirkus later said. "It was the normal tone almost like he was crying.…I just wasn't sure what he said so I asked him to repeat it."

Mathis obliged: "Someone has shot my family."[1]

Kirkus hung up the phone, glanced at the clock, dressed, put on his bulletproof vest and headed out the door.

In the forty years since the call, Kirkus has relived that night and the months that followed countless times. It was perhaps the most infamous murder case in South Dakota's history. A thirty-year-old mother was shot twice in the head at point-blank range. Two of her three children, ages

South Dakota's Mathis Murders

The Mathis farm where the murders occurred is eight miles north of Mount Vernon and one mile east. Mount Vernon is approximately twelve miles west of Mitchell. *Courtesy of Allison Carpenter.*

two and four, were also shot in the head. Her infant third child escaped the carnage because he was staying with his grandparents.

The murders have never been solved. No longer even a "cold case," it's nevertheless been frozen in Kirkus's mind since that Tuesday, September 8, 1981.

A county road, 397th Avenue, extends north from Mount Vernon, a small farming community in east central South Dakota. The land is flat, the soil rich and dark. When rain is adequate, crops are as plentiful as anywhere in the heartland. Named after the home of America's first president, it lies some twelve miles west of the World's Only Corn Palace in Mitchell and eighty miles west of Sioux Falls, the state's largest city. After alerting the Mitchell Police Department dispatcher of the need for an ambulance and backup, Kirkus started for the Mathis farm, eight miles north and a mile east.

Driving at speeds approaching one hundred miles an hour, Kirkus slowed when he met a semi-tractor-trailer. He wrote down the license number as it passed, then resumed speed.

As Kirkus neared the farm's driveway, he glanced at his watch: 4:07 a.m. He also noted headlights approaching from the east. Kirkus scanned the layout of the farm, seeing a house on the left and a large, metal machine shed straight ahead. He doused the headlights of his patrol car, not knowing if the assailant was still on the property.

"If somebody had shot his family…I had no idea that somebody wasn't running around out in the farm yet and I turned off the lights. I didn't want someone shooting at me."[2]

A pickup truck then entered the yard and parked close to the machine shed where the Mathis family was living while their new home was being built. When the driver exited the truck, Kirkus saw that it was Vern Mathis, John's father.

"What's going on?" the elder Mathis asked Kirkus.

The John Mathis farm, eight miles north and one mile east of Mount Vernon. *Courtesy of the Davison County Sheriff's Department.*

South Dakota's Mathis Murders

Aerial view of the John Mathis farm. *Courtesy of the Davison County Sheriff's Department.*

"I don't know," Kirkus responded.

Then, in the glow of the pickup's headlights, they saw three words written in gold spray paint on the shed's large sliding door: "Mathus suck shit."[3]

Kirkus, grabbing his riot shotgun, saw that Vern Mathis was also carrying a rifle or shotgun. The two men approached the building.

When Kirkus opened the walk-in door, he saw John Mathis kneeling at the foot of a bed. Kirkus approached the bed and saw blood on the corner of the sheet that was covering a body. He then saw two other beds adjacent to the first, both containing bodies. All three bodies were covered. Kirkus pulled back the bedcovers so he could check for a pulse.

Dead from apparent gunshot wounds were Ladonna Mathis, wife of John Mathis, and two of their sons: Brian, four, and Patrick, two. Ladonna had been shot once in the head and once in the neck, Patrick twice in the head and Brian once in the head.

The bodies were still warm to the touch, and Kirkus saw that the wounds appeared to be caused by small-caliber slugs.[4]

Horror in the Heartland

Left: Ladonna Gerlach, age twenty-three, when she was engaged to be married to John Mathis. *Courtesy of Marilyn Reimnitz.*

Right: Murdered children Brian, age four, and Patrick, age two. *Courtesy of Marilyn Reimnitz.*

Kirkus helped Mathis up from the foot of Ladonna's bed. Mathis complained that his left arm hurt, and Kirkus noted that it was wrapped in a pink long-sleeved shirt. Kirkus observed a hole in the shirt and saw powder burns around the hole. He pulled back the sleeve and saw an entrance wound on the inside of Mathis's left forearm. He also checked the outer part of Mathis's arm and saw a small bulge, which appeared to be an exit wound. Kirkus took a package of bandages from his trauma kit, dressed the wound and began treating Mathis for shock.

Kirkus then asked Mathis what had occurred.

"I'll get that son-of-a-bitch," Mathis said, and Kirkus asked for a description.

"A person wearing dark clothing—dark colored clothing and wearing a deal over his face," Mathis replied. Then Mathis said that "none of this would have happened" if he had locked the door.[5]

Chapter 2
INVESTIGATION

Davison County sheriff Lyle Swenson pulled into the Mathis driveway at 4:25 a.m., shortly after the ambulance. A lawman with thirty years of experience, Swenson started as a deputy sheriff in 1951; he was elected sheriff in 1954 and continued in that position—often unopposed—until 1997, when he was appointed U.S. marshal. Swenson was followed ten minutes later by Deputy Brad Bortnem, who transported Vern Mathis to Methodist Hospital, where his son John had been taken by the ambulance for treatment of his arm wound.

Despite his long tenure in law enforcement, Swenson knew this case required resources his department lacked. Personnel from the state Division of Criminal Investigation arrived later that morning. The Mitchell Police Department offered its services as well, and Swenson would also turn to the FBI for assistance; such was the complexity of the case. Later, assistance would come from an unexpected and controversial source: a New Jersey psychic.

Two central questions quickly presented themselves to Swenson and Kirkus: Who was the mysterious "hooded masked man" described by John Mathis? And what possible motive would explain the killing of a thirty-year-old farm wife and her two small sons?

Nearly from the outset, Swenson was suspicious of John Mathis's version of events. On the day of the murders, he told the *Daily Republic* in Mitchell that he had talked to Mathis. "He doesn't know who did it, but he says someone else did, not himself. We have not been able to prove or disprove it. The man is in shock."

Horror in the Heartland

Longtime Davison County sheriff Lyle Swenson. *Courtesy of the* Daily Republic.

Law enforcement began to comb the Mathis farm, searching for the murder weapon. Fifteen men performed a dragnet of the buildings and the land surrounding them, seeking a .22-caliber rifle that investigators believed was used in the shootings. No gun was found, nor were Swenson and other investigators able to find evidence pointing to any suspect, even after a full day of intense investigation.

Said Swenson, "It's just got us puzzled. Nothing seems to fit. Sometimes we think we got something, then we are starting from scratch."[6]

Meanwhile, Kirkus and DCI agent Ken Giegling of Chamberlain questioned Mathis, age thirty, while he was recovering at the Methodist Hospital in Mitchell. They advised him of his Miranda rights, and he waived them for the interview.

Mathis said that sometime after two in the morning, his son Patrick awakened and said he had to go potty. Mathis said he took his son to urinate in a pail inside the shed, got him a drink of water and tucked him into bed. Mathis said he then went outdoors into some trees to relieve himself and heard his dog, Spotty, barking in a nearby building. He let the dog out and walked to a farrowing barn to check on a sow that had given birth to baby pigs earlier that day. When Mathis left the barn, he heard Spotty barking again, so he went to tie him up. It was then he thought he heard an engine running but couldn't identify the location. He pushed Spotty into the doghouse and walked toward the shed where his family was sleeping.[7]

As Mathis approached the corner of the machine shed, a man closed the walk-in door and started for him. The man was carrying a rifle. "I'll get you," Mathis remembered the man saying.

Mathis reached for the barrel of the rifle. He missed, and the gun evidently went off. He said his arm felt like it had puffed up. Mathis said he swung at the intruder but did not know if he hit him. The man made a loud noise "like they teach you in basic training when attacking a dummy with a rifle and bayonet," Mathis said.

SOUTH DAKOTA'S MATHIS MURDERS

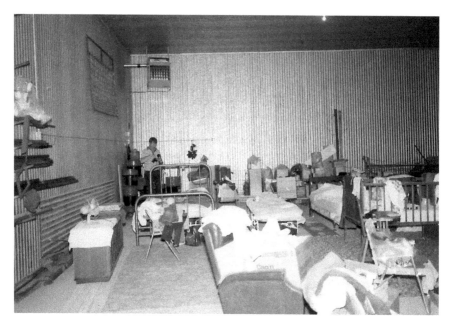

Interior of the temporary home in the machine shed where Ladonna Mathis, Brian and Patrick were shot on September 8, 1981. *Courtesy of the Davison County Sheriff's Department.*

When asked to repeat the story, Mathis added some details about when he called Doug Kirkus and his father, Vern. Mathis said he had no idea who the killer was and denied that he had killed his own family. Kirkus and Giegling told Mathis there was no evidence to support his story about a hooded masked man, but Mathis "calmly answered that he had not shot his family."[8]

As the interview ended, Mathis was asked if he could think of any other details. After a moment, he said that the mask on the killer had a lighter-colored trim around the holes for the eyes and mouth, but he could not recall what color it was.

Although Mathis agreed to submit to hypnosis as one way to recall more details of the incident and said he would be willing to take a polygraph test, neither occurred.

The next day, Wednesday, the search intensified for the small-caliber gun used in the killings. It was presumed to be a .22-caliber rifle, based on the recovery of the bullets fired into the victims, who were found in three of the four beds placed side by side in the machine shed. Ladonna Mathis's bed was closest to the walk-in door, then Patrick's and Brian's. The closest bed was empty, and a crib stood near the foot of Ladonna's bed.

The coroner's report described a considerable amount of blood on the bedding of each victim from the head wounds, but "there was no evidence of a struggle in the immediate area," suggesting that the victims were killed as they slept. Davison County Coroner George Bittner said all three victims were in their nightclothes, and no bruises were found that could have indicated a struggle. "It apparently happened very fast," Bittner said.[9]

Outside the machine shed, the Davison County Sheriff's Department, the state DCI and other agencies searched the land and nine buildings, seeking the murder weapon. The ninety-degree heat intensified the work, especially the partial excavation of a hog manure tank. Two septic tanks containing hog waste were searched, with no findings.

The agents also looked closely at the partially constructed house that was being built to replace the Mathis home, which had been destroyed in a fire caused by a lightning strike on July 22. An earlier fire, on July 9, had damaged the home. Following the September 8 killings, a $50,000 insurance claim paid to the Mathis family for the fires was being reevaluated, and

Exterior of the machine shed that served as a temporary home for the John Mathis family. Obscene graffiti, "Mathus suck shit," appeared on the right-side sliding door. *Courtesy of the Davison County Sheriff's Department.*

the second fire was considered an open case, according to a Farm Bureau Insurance spokesman from Huron.[10]

The search continued Thursday but produced little evidence, and Swenson, frustrated by the failure to find the murder weapon, urged the use of the Secret Witness phone line.

The following day, Friday, September 11, about 350 people, including John Mathis, attended the funeral for Ladonna and her two children. Mathis had been released from the hospital, under doctor's orders to return for further treatment of his arm wound. Though law enforcement now considered him a person of interest, no charges had been filed against him.

The Salem Lutheran Church in Mount Vernon was filled to overflowing, and many were forced to the basement to hear the service on speakers.

"If death did not harm your Lord it will not harm you," the Reverend Eugene Roesler told the gathering.

He later related to the press: "Really, on this occasion, God is our only hope." He called the deaths unexplainable and mysterious.

A sheriff's deputy and an agent from the state DCI stood on the sidewalk outside the church before the service, then entered before it began. Some family members, angered at the presence of the media, threatened reporters and photographers who tried to get close to the church. A fifty-four-car procession accompanied the caskets to the cemetery outside of town.[11]

At that moment, on the Mathis farm, authorities expanded the search for the murder weapon, using horses to comb land within a three-mile radius of the farm, but the effort produced nothing of value. Sheriff Swenson promised to continue the search, because "we've got to be missing something."

Then, eight days after the slayings, with no murder weapon found and the search warrant about to expire, Swenson, Davison County state's attorney Pat Kiner and others involved in the investigation met to decide if the warrant needed to be extended. What started as a search of the machine shed and other buildings nearby, then land within a three-mile radius of the farm, was later extended to nearby farms. Investigators decided to go over the area again. With the warrant extended, the search was renewed, not just for the .22-caliber gun but also the can of spray paint that was used to write "Mathus suck shit" on the machine shed door. The extra days produced little, and Swenson acknowledged on September 23, nearly two weeks after the murders, that "we're not much further than we were before."[12]

With the warrant expired and John Mathis released from the hospital, Swenson looked for help in an unusual place: a New Jersey psychic named

Horror in the Heartland

Supported by his father, Vern, on his right, John Mathis, with his arm in a sling, attends the funeral of his wife, Ladonna, and two sons, Brian, four, and Patrick, two, at the Salem Lutheran Church in Mount Vernon. *Courtesy of the Daily Republic.*

Vern Mathis Sr. *(left)* and his son John leave the church following the funeral of Ladonna Mathis and sons Brian and Patrick. *Courtesy of the Davison County Sheriff's Department.*

Dorothy Allison, fifty-six. She said she had seen the face of a man who she believed killed Ladonna, Brian and Patrick.

"Whatever I've been telling them (law enforcement) they've been finding," Allison said of her involvement in the case. Sheriff Swenson called her for help on September 17, after talking with a police friend of hers in New Jersey.[13]

Allison said that after Swenson told her of the unsolved triple murder, she knew almost instantly how the victims had died. She said that by concentrating, she got a mental picture of a killing and then passed along the clues to authorities. She wouldn't reveal all she had seen in her visions, such as a description of the killer or his reasons for the murders. But she did believe the killer's name had a capital "M" in it, and the numbers 5, 6 and 9 were important. The victims knew the killer, she said, and the stock of the gun used was burned.[14] Allison said she was studying pictures of the Mathis family so she could intrude on the thoughts of the killer. The psychic said she never let a killer go.

"When I get a killer, I feel great," Allison said. She claimed to have nabbed fourteen since 1977. The New Jersey housewife said that, since 1968, only four cases she had taken on remained unsolved, and the effectiveness of her help depended on how authorities used her tips. Allison's psychic powers have been used to help authorities solve some famous cases, including that of Patty Hearst, daughter of media mogul William Randolph Hearst Jr., who was kidnapped by the Symbiones Liberation Army in 1974.[15] Allison said she would like to visit Mount Vernon because of her interest in solving the case. Swenson said he and his department welcomed Allison's help and would continue to work with her. At the same time, the FBI was compiling a psychological profile to determine what type of person could commit such a crime.

With the investigation at the Mathis farm now nearly exhausted, authorities turned to a new phase in the case. Attorney General Mark Meierhenry believed there was enough evidence to empanel a grand jury, and his request was granted on October 2, a Friday, by Circuit Judge George Wuest. The grand jury would meet the following Wednesday and hear testimony from witnesses connected to the case. State's attorney Pat Kiner explained the role of the grand jury at a press conference. He said it could assist in the investigation by hearing testimony, asking for additional evidence and suggesting additional avenues of inquiry for authorities.

There had been no arrests since the September 8 murders. John Mathis, who was shot in the left forearm during the murders, had been a person of interest in the case, but neither Kiner nor Swenson would say if Mathis was the subject of the grand jury probe. Mathis had refused to talk to authorities since the day the killings occurred. He retained Gregory, South Dakota attorney Wally Eklund while he was in the hospital recovering from the bullet wound he said he sustained in the struggle.

On the same day as the announcement of the grand jury, the Mathis family offered a $10,000 reward for information leading to the arrest and conviction of the person or persons responsible for the murders. In addition to the reward, the family distributed notices to Mitchell businesses explaining the reward and named Gerrit Brink, former sheriff of Aurora County, as the person to contact with any information.

And, in a startling revelation, Davison County sheriff Swenson told the *Argus Leader* on October 3 that New Jersey psychic Dorothy Allison had told him the name of the person who killed Ladonna Mathis and her sons. However, Swenson refused to reveal the person's identity. Swenson said that Allison told him she had seen the killer's face in a vision before she received a photograph of the Mathis family.

Chapter 3

INDICTMENT

Attorney General Meierhenry told reporters on Wednesday, October 14, that "electrifying evidence" had been presented to grand jurors that morning, evidence provided by DCI agent Ken Giegling of Chamberlain. Meierhenry would not provide details of the evidence but said, "It brings us a lot closer to finding the person who perpetrated these killings."[16]

Sequestered in a third-floor room of the Davison County Courthouse, the grand jurors would hear additional evidence from all persons who viewed the crime area and those with knowledge about the aftermath. Grand jurors were shown a videotape of the scene by Andy Comer of the DCI, and they heard testimony from state deputy fire marshal Pat Harrington and Mount Vernon fire chief Jerry Giedd, who investigated the fires on July 9 and July 22 that first damaged and then destroyed the Mathis home. In coming days, other witnesses would be called, including the Mathis family babysitter, neighbors and members of the Mathis family. John Mathis, who had returned to the family farm after his release from the hospital, would also be called to testify, accompanied by his attorney, Wally Eklund. Jurors were still awaiting evidence that Meierhenry had sent to the FBI lab in Washington, D.C. Meierhenry said the initial test results showed a need for further tests.

On Friday, October 30, John Mathis was indicted on three counts of first-degree murder and arrested by sheriff's deputy Kirkus at a local restaurant. He was taken to Judge Wuest's courtroom, where Wuest asked

Top: The Davison County Courthouse, where early hearings were held in the John Mathis murder case. *Author's photo.*

Bottom: The courtroom on third floor of the Davison County Courthouse where Circuit Judge George Wuest presided. Wuest later stepped aside, and the Mathis trial was moved to Yankton County. *Author's photo.*

him to approach the bench. Dressed in a blue flannel shirt and blue jeans, his left arm still in a sling, Mathis gave brief answers to questions from Wuest, who then ordered him to be bound over on a $200,000 cash bond, even though no bond was recommended by Meierhenry.[17]

Mathis left the courtroom flanked by Swenson and Kirkus and was escorted to the fourth-floor jail. Earlier in the morning, the grand jury had deliberated for an hour and fifteen minutes before handing its verdict to the attorney general. They had been meeting for five-and-a-half days following their October 7 empanelment and had heard from twenty witnesses.[18]

John Mathis, right, is escorted into the Davison County Courthouse on October 30, 1981, by Deputy Sheriff Doug Kirkus. *Courtesy of the* Sioux Falls Argus Leader.

Meierhenry asked the court not to dismiss the grand jury, saying that there might be other criminal activity tied to the case beyond the Mathis indictment. Mathis's attorney, Eklund, while acknowledging that "you're never fully prepared for anything like this," said the indictment did not come as a complete surprise. He said a change of venue would be considered.

With the indictment now in place, Mathis, if convicted, was facing life imprisonment or the death penalty. He and his attorney were already planning their next move, and by the afternoon, they made it, filing an affidavit asking for a new judge. In the affidavit, Mathis stated he didn't think he could get a fair and impartial trial with Wuest presiding.

"I was told the defendant didn't want anybody from Mitchell on it," said Wuest, the presiding judge in the state's Fourth Judicial Circuit. Wuest said the next most senior judge in the circuit, Thomas Anderst of Madison, must decide which other judge should hear the case.[19] Before Mathis was indicted, Meierhenry had said the usual procedure was for the chief circuit judge—in this case, George Wuest—to assign the judge who would hear the case. Both the defense and the state can for one time and for no reason request the removal of a judge from a case, Meierhenry said. Wuest confirmed on Saturday that Anderst would preside over the Mathis case going forward.

One of Judge Anderst's first decisions was to release John Mathis on a $300,000 property bond, replacing the $200,000 cash bond originally approved by Judge Wuest. Meierhenry had no objection to the new bond, saying the property put up was worth twice the cash bond amount. But Anderst imposed a number of conditions on Mathis in addition to the bond. He was not to communicate with the James Tatum family or the Lorenz Gerlach family without his attorney present, and he could make no physical changes to buildings on the farm. Kim Tatum, daughter of James Tatum, was the Mathis family babysitter. Lorenz and Evelyn Gerlach are the parents of Mathis's murdered wife, Ladonna, and they were caring for his son, Duane, eight months, who had been staying with them when the killings occurred. Anderst also ordered Mathis to live with his father, Vern, who was ordered to supervise his son, make certain he appeared in court and report if he broke the law or left the jurisdiction while free on bond.[20]

Meanwhile, the state was preparing a motion to enable a further search of the Mathis farm and to conduct a sound test, which Meierhenry said was to "fire a gun." He said he wanted to complete the test before snow covered the ground, which could affect the test results. Anderst denied the motion for a search warrant but allowed the sound tests by approving an oral motion for discovery. The state team fired a .22 rifle from five locations on the farm.

Circuit Court judge George Wuest. Wuest called a special grand jury to hear evidence in the murders of Ladonna Mathis and sons Brian and Patrick. He later was replaced by Judge Thomas Anderst after John Mathis asked for a new judge. Wuest went on to become a state supreme court justice. *Courtesy of the Davison County Clerk of Courts.*

For weeks, the Mathis defense team had been considering asking the court to change the location of the trial, believing that media coverage had made it difficult if not impossible to seat jurors who would be impartial toward John Mathis. Eklund had formally filed a motion in early November, but the month ended with no decision from the bench. Finally, on Wednesday, December 9, Anderst announced the trial would be moved. He said he had looked at both Yankton and Watertown because they fit the requirements for a trial and had vacant courtrooms.

Meierhenry wasn't surprised. "I anticipated there would be a change of venue," he said. "It's to a place that's close enough that will not cause a lot of inconvenience. I'm glad it wasn't moved to the western part of the state," which was Mathis and Eklund's goal.[21]

Anderst set the trial date for February 1 in Yankton County, but it wasn't long before Mathis, unsatisfied with the Yankton location for the trial, tested the water for yet a different location. Eklund requested an additional sixty days to study whether the trial should be moved again. "I already heard your first (change of venue) motion and granted it," the judge said in rejecting the motion. But he did approve the request by Eklund and his law partner, Charles "Rick" Johnson, to see evidence tested at the state and FBI laboratories. Meierhenry said he was still waiting for FBI tests on a .22-caliber rifle shell casing found in Mathis's pocket at Methodist Hospital on the morning of the killings. Anderst's ruling also allowed the defense to hear several hours of tape recordings made with Kim Tatum, the Mathis family babysitter and helper with chores.

While the attorneys were jockeying for an advantage in pretrial motions, the residents of Mount Vernon were watching the developments closely, and some were unhappy that the three murders had put their town on the map.

"It's changed the town as much as it's changed the neighbors," said Buzzy, a short, stocky and talkative man who owned the only Mount Vernon saloon.

"They're scared," said Buzzy's tablemate, Don. "I wouldn't want to go out there, you might get shot at. Most of 'em won't even leave their places after dark."[22]

Their efforts to get the trial moved a second time stymied, the defense succeeded in obtaining a six-week delay in the trial's start time, from February 1 to March 15, citing test evidence that had not yet been returned from the FBI. The defense was working on its own tests of the shell casings and clothing worn by John Mathis and needed time to compare the findings, said Johnson, who said the case "has more complications than any other murder trial I have heard of in the country."

February met two expectations: cold weather and a spate of motions by John Mathis's defense team. At the end of January, Judge Anderst had denied a motion to suppress evidence obtained from John Mathis's clothing on the morning of the murders. Eklund wanted the live .22-caliber rifle shell found in Mathis's pocket at Methodist Hospital excluded as evidence, arguing that the search was unconstitutional. The judge disagreed, pointing out that Mathis knowingly and willfully allowed the agent to discuss the incident with him and that Mathis himself had called law enforcement to the scene—and that further, at the time of the bullet's discovery, Mathis was not a suspect.

Davison County deputy sheriff Doug Kirkus drove this department 1980 Chevrolet Impala to the crime scene on September 8, 1981. *Courtesy of Doug Kirkus.*

Other motions were pending, including one to have the case dismissed and another to have the case moved from Yankton to another city. Still another motion asked for the defense to have triple the allowed number of twenty peremptory challenges to potential jurors.

Those motions, though of public interest, were overshadowed by the news that Meierhenry would seek the death penalty if John Mathis was convicted of killing his wife and two of his sons.

Eklund confirmed that Meierhenry had advised him by letter weeks before that the death penalty would be sought, and he said he had sought Meierhenry's view because "it would be awfully unfair to our client not to know."

In 1980, thirty-six states, including South Dakota, allowed capital punishment. In 1979, Governor Bill Janklow signed into law the state's death penalty statute. The state had executed ten men between its admission in 1889 and the abolition of the death penalty in 1915. The death penalty was reinstated in 1939 and used only once before the U.S. Supreme Court declared capital punishment "cruel and unusual." However, South Dakota and many other states tweaked laws to address the high court's concerns.[23]

Defense attorney Rick Johnson said Meierhenry's decision to seek the death penalty came as no surprise. "He rather threatened that from the time he got involved. So no, it was no surprise. We don't have to be stupid to know what he had in mind. Then there is Lyle Swenson with his comments. I think the bodies were still warm yet when he said somebody would burn."[24]

Johnson also said he would seek a closed hearing to discuss two issues related to the case: news coverage and the death penalty. "The television coverage has been worse than newspaper coverage," he said. "So we want tapes of those telecasts, not just the transcripts."

As February came to a close, the defense team for John Mathis had not yet received written results of the FBI tests on evidence, prompting Judge Anderst to grant another delay in the trial, until April 12.

Meierhenry resisted the second delay, unsuccessfully arguing that the defense had had access to the blood sample evidence for more than a month, "thus there is no show for need of a continuance." While Anderst ruled favorably on the later date for the trial, he closed the doors on news media for a pretrial hearing on procedure. Defense attorney Johnson had asked for the closed hearing, saying "We have definite objections about some of the discussion of the death penalty and we have some procedural matters to work out. With the press present, it could be highly prejudicial so we asked the judge to discuss the matter in chambers or in a court with the press excluded." Meierhenry said he didn't object to the closed hearing, but later added, "I didn't ask to have anybody thrown out."[25]

March brought two key developments in the case. The defense received the written test results from the FBI, which had been the central reason for the trial's second delay, and Judge Anderst denied the defense's motion to move the trial from Yankton to Rapid City. Anderst, after reviewing media coverage of the case, including TV tapes, ruled that the defense had failed to prove Mathis could not get a fair trial in Yankton.

Chapter 4

WHO WAS JOHN MATHIS?

By all accounts, John Wayne Mathis was a hardworking farmer who had a close relationship with his father, Vern. Many who knew him said he worked "all the time" and that it wasn't unusual for him to be in the field at two or three o'clock in the morning.

Born on July 25, 1951, in Mitchell, Mathis was the middle child of Vern and Pearl Mathis. Vern Jr. was his older brother and Norma Jean his younger sister. As a youth, Mathis attended country school, then four years of high school in Mount Vernon.

Mathis met his wife, Ladonna Gerlach, at a dance in Mitchell, and they married on May 4, 1973. A wedding photo shows two beaming newlyweds, the bride wearing a gown of white organza and carrying a bouquet of yellow roses and white carnations. Her husband, smiling broadly, is wearing a dark suit and tie and horn-rimmed glasses. Their life seemed to be set on a course focused on hard work, success and family.

A news story before the trial began described Mathis as a Lutheran and a Republican who voted for Ronald Reagan. For fun and to unwind, he fished, bowled and danced. Asked if he was a religious man, Mathis said: "Not as much as some think they are." But then he added that he had turned to prayer. "I hope it helps," he said.[26]

The pastor of the Lutheran Church that the Mathises attended, Eugene Roesler, said he didn't feel that "Mathis had a very good home life when he was growing up." He doubted there was "a great deal of affection" in the family.[27]

Defense attorney Wally Eklund (*left*) and defendant John Mathis. *Courtesy of the* Daily Republic.

Interviews with neighbors all painted the same picture: John had few, if any, close friends. His wife was active in church affairs, but John was always busy on the farm, often working late at night.[28]

Ironically, the deputy he called on the morning of the murders was his classmate, Doug Kirkus, who lived in Mount Vernon. They graduated from high school in 1970, two of twenty-seven in the class.

"John wasn't involved in anything," Kirkus remembers. "He came to school and after school he was expected to go home and work. He wasn't in sports or band. I wouldn't say John was a loner, but he didn't participate in extra-curricular. He wasn't one to go out and party."

Mathis's work ethic came from his father. "The family was run by an iron fist," said Sheriff Swenson. "Vern senior was a dictator. His father, Irving, they said was a first-class dictator. The gal that married Vern, his ex-wife and second wife, came to my front door at 10 at night, the day of the murders" with information about Vern. Swenson said he used some of the information to create a profile for the FBI.

Marilyn Reimnitz, Ladonna's younger sister, said she did not like Vern Mathis. "Vernon wanted her to do something and she said something and he was unhappy about it. It didn't sit right with him, but I can't prove it," Marilyn said.

However, Marilyn said her parents, Lorenz and Evelyn Gerlach, liked the man their daughter had married. "Not that John wasn't a favorite. My mom and dad loved him as a son-in-law. He had quirks. Nothing was important but to get out there and work."

Following the September 8, 1981, slayings, Doug Kirkus was deposed by Mathis's attorneys, Wally Eklund and Rick Johnson. Kirkus told them he knew Mathis "fairly well." Asked to characterize Mathis, Kirkus said he was "always a fairly quiet, very hard-working individual." In high school, Mathis was not a "fighter" and never got into trouble, Kirkus said.

"Was John, during your high school era there, ever known to be a boozer or make use of drugs or anything like this?" Eklund asked.

"No," Kirkus responded.

During an interview on September 12, four days after the murders, neighbors told Kirkus and DCI agent Giegling that they could not recall the Mathises having any close friends, but they did say that Ladonna was "active in church affairs." The neighbors both commented "on how busy John was on the farm and often working late into the night."

Another neighbor said in an interview with DCI agent Dave Muller and Sheriff Swenson that "he had known the Mathis family all his life and that he knew Vern's father and said that Vern was very much like his father, Irving. "Vern Sr.'s father, Irving, had four boys and…all four boys were raised in an environment where work was the dominant force. All four boys had trouble getting their wives settled down to the way of life which was expected of them," the interview and subsequent report of the interview said. "A woman in the Mathis house was expected to do more than the average woman was expected to do," the report quoted the neighbor as saying.[29]

John Mathis's best man at his wedding and best friend in high school, Lyle Reimnitz, agreed with the description set forth during depositions and the trial. "Neither one of us played sports," Reimnitz said. "Farming was our major interest. He was a very hard worker, dedicated. Maybe it was his downfall. There are other things in life besides work."

John Mathis with his sons; from left, Brian, Duane and Patrick. *Courtesy of the Davison County Sheriff's Department.*

"His father was dominating," Reimnitz went on. "John said if he came home late from a date, his dad would meet him by the gate and told him you've got so much time to get here and go to work."

Mathis's defense team and its expert witnesses portrayed Mathis as "slow" intellectually and said he would have been incapable of planning the murders.

A psychological evaluation in March 1982 by Thomas L. Jackson, a licensed psychologist referred by Rick Johnson, summarized Mathis's scores at 79 for verbal IQ, 88 for performance IQ, and full-scale or total IQ at 81. Mathis scored low in verbal memory, words and ability to work with abstract symbols. But he did much better in nonverbal areas, such as hands-on reasoning and visual problem solving. Mathis's scores would place him in the "low average" category of the current Wechsler intelligence scale.[30]

"I would not say he was dumb except book learning," Reimnitz said. "Shop was his favorite class, and mine too. He knew more about welding than our shop teacher did. After he was married, he put a turbo charger on the tractor. He took an old cow barn and remodeled it into a farrowing barn."

Reimnitz said he thought Mathis was probably a C student in English and math, "but anything shop related, or farming, in my mind that took some clear thinking and planning. He could do things."

When they graduated from high school, Reimnitz invited his friend to his house southwest of Mount Vernon to celebrate because no event was being held at the Mathis home.

After graduation, Mathis joined the National Guard, and Reimnitz signed up two weeks later, but they were in different units. Reimnitz said it was a good experience for both men. "It went fine, no trouble. It was a step forward when he got out."

For the five-foot-ten, 155-pound Mathis, hard work was a way of life and a common denominator for the two friends. To unwind, they attended dances, which was where Mathis met his future wife. They went on bowling dates, too. And it wasn't long before Mathis was urging Reimnitz to ask Ladonna's younger sister, Marilyn, for a date. Lyle and Marilyn married in 1975, two years after John and Ladonna.

After the trial, Reimnitz avoided all contact with Mathis.

"I don't talk to him," Reimnitz said in 2020. "I saw him years ago. I avoid him like you would the plague. The last time I spoke to him was when he came to Lorenz and Evelyn's house" to pick up his son, Duane, then an infant.

"If I see him, I go the other way."

As does Dwight Gerlach, Mathis's brother-in-law and the older brother of Ladonna Mathis. But it wasn't always that way.

"We had our Christmases, Thanksgivings, birthdays and maybe anniversaries. They came as a family. There was never any squabbles or silent moments when you felt stressed. The only thing I remember is going up there [to the Mathis farm]. I farm all day. I don't need to farm at night. And we'd have to go out in the dark and take a look at a piece of machinery."

After Mathis was acquitted, he was allowed to take custody of his infant son, Duane, who had been in the care of Ladonna's parents. Gerlach was there that day. "I had to hand him, Duane, over. I had him in my arms and handed him to John. My mom and dad couldn't have done it."

Gerlach admits he and the family were "cold" to Mathis after the trial. They were put off, not only by the trial's outcome, but by some of the questions that Mathis posed about his deceased family when they met in the church library. "He made comments, like, 'Do you think they are OK,' or something about 'where they were at.'

"Sometimes it's better to be silent than to talk. You keep your distance."

Chapter 5

A BATTLE OF TITANS

Call it a coincidence or some sort of cosmic destiny: the John Mathis murder case pitted two of the state's premier trial lawyers against each other.

In itself, this wouldn't be unusual because a high-profile capital case naturally would be prosecuted by the state's top law enforcement lawyer: the attorney general. And if the accused in such a case wanted to ensure his best chance at acquittal, he would retain one of the preeminent defense attorneys available.

This case, however, had an added dimension. The face-off between the state's attorney general, Mark Meierhenry, and well-known Gregory lawyer Charles "Rick" Johnson was a media dream. The two men were friends and grew up in the same town. They played football together, Johnson at guard and Meierhenry at tackle, though Johnson was two years older. They took different paths to becoming lawyers and remained friends over the years, though the murder trial severely strained that friendship—not because of both men's competitiveness or the grisly nature of the case, but because it became personal.

In October 1979, Meierhenry and a friend, state treasurer David Volk, went pheasant hunting, and later in the day, they stopped by a Winner tavern. They discovered a blackjack game in the rear of the bar and tried their luck. News reporters found out, and Meierhenry and Volk later pleaded guilty to a misdemeanor. Gambling was illegal in South Dakota at the time—and would be until 1989, when casino gambling was legalized in Deadwood. That door was opened in 1986, when voters approved a state-operated lottery.

During the Mathis trial, Johnson referred to Meierhenry's use of the word "odds," suggesting that the attorney general liked games of chance and saying that a trial involving a man's guilt or innocence should not be characterized in such a manner. Meierhenry, who had not made that comparison, was incensed at the reference and condemned it during his closing arguments.

Then there was the discovery of a spent .22-caliber cartridge by jurors when they were returning from supper the first day of deliberations. Some thought that the casing was a plant, intended to influence the jury because it would support the defense's contention that .22-caliber shells were commonly found anywhere in South Dakota. The defense bristled at the implication that it was involved, and the incident further strained the friendship between Meierhenry and Johnson.

Eklund, Johnson's partner in the Gregory firm and cocounsel in the Mathis trial, said in a late 2020 interview that the two men had patched up their differences. "They were good friends," Eklund said. "It took awhile, but I think they came around."

Johnson came by his interest in the law naturally. His father, George, was a prominent attorney in the state and his son carried on the firm's reputation for excellence. "As far as ability, Rick was one of two or three top defense trial lawyers in the state at the time," said retired Pierre attorney Charles Thompson, a noted lawyer in his own right. "Rick was extremely competent with a jury. He was absolutely good at picking a jury and relating to a jury. He could understand their mindset going in and of course he would try to bring out his point that would resonate well with the jurors."

Another characteristic of Johnson, and one recognized by both his fellow attorneys and the public, was his courage. "Rick would defend anything and take it to trial if he couldn't get it worked out. He had absolutely no fear to try a jury case, and if he lost, he'd take it to appeal. Rick was really, really good. He kicked the crap out of me several times," Thompson said.

At the time of the trial, when asked his opinion of the two adversaries, Governor Bill Janklow said Johnson was "as good as anybody I know. He's bright, competent, honest and incredibly versed in the law."[31] And that praise was from a man who was friends with Mark Meierhenry and recruited him to run for attorney general.

Even Meierhenry himself had only praise for Johnson. "I'm going against a lawyer that is much more skilled: the legendary Rick Johnson," Meierhenry said.

Madison attorney and retired circuit court judge David Gienapp was a good friend of Johnson's and tried several cases with him. He said Johnson displayed innovation in his approach to the law. "He and I had one case and by the time it ended, the statute of limitations had run out. But he was able to develop a case showing fraud by the other party. So the statute of limitations wasn't in force." Gienapp recalls Johnson being creative in other ways, too. Instead of hiring an expensive, out-of-state expert on mechanical issues, for example, "he would find a local mechanic."

Defense attorney Rick Johnson. *Courtesy of the Johnson family.*

Gienapp remembers watching Johnson in the courtroom. "He would be aggressive when he had to, but juries seemed to like him. His intuition seemed good. I always joked that with one arm, he couldn't go long without dropping a legal pad," something other attorneys and courtroom observers noticed as well. Johnson was born with the lower part of his left arm missing, from the elbow down.

"But I played golf and racquetball with him and he had no problem," Gienapp said, chuckling.

In Meierhenry, however, Johnson was up against an equally talented lawyer. The bespectacled Meierhenry had a reputation for thoroughness and preparation. If Johnson was good at understanding a jury, so was Meierhenry. "Mark did the same thing on the prosecution side," Thompson said. "He was very, very thorough."

And Meierhenry and Johnson shared yet another trait that made them formidable courtroom foes. "They were good storytellers," Thompson said. "They would start out their case by trying to put together a story—how do we do this, as a book or a novel or whatever. An outline of how to see it. They were really good communicators. Rick's final arguments were very plain and forceful. Meierhenry was a little smoother. Both were spellbinding."

Both Johnson and Meierhenry had help. Meierhenry had the attorney general's resources, including Dennis Holmes, assistant attorney general and assistant prosecutor. Eklund, who shared the defense duties, was the first to be retained when Vern Mathis Sr. contacted his law office. Eklund and his family were returning from a vacation at Lewis and Clark Lake near Yankton and heard a report of the murders on the radio. The next day, he connected with the Mathises, starting a months-long association.

Defense attorney Wally Eklund. *Courtesy of the Johnson family.*

Eklund, who grew up on a ranch north of Wood in Mellette County, ended his legal career by serving as a circuit court judge for seven years. He first became interested in the law because his family had been represented by George Johnson, Rick's father. When Eklund was still in law school at the University of South Dakota, he interned at the Johnson law firm; in 1971, he moved to Gregory to join the firm.

"I tried my first jury trial a week after I took the bar," Eklund said in December 2020. "I represented a young dairy farmer in Hutchinson County. It was a breach of contract case." Eklund won the case.

Eklund and Johnson normally didn't team up to defend a client. "I can only think of four or five where we were in the courtroom at the same time," Eklund said. "Usually in criminal cases people have trouble affording one lawyer, let alone two.

"Obviously it was a pretty damn serious case, three people dead, two little boys and a wife," Eklund said, explaining why he and his partner both defended Mathis.

And Eklund was acquainted with Meierhenry. "I knew Mark pretty well when he was in legal aid out in Rosebud. We tried a jury trial together in Mellette County one time."

With Meierhenry, Eklund said, "You are in a battle."

Thompson remembers that Eklund was "not as flashy as Rick, and a little more of a bookworm.

"Wally was solid in every way. He was steady, a get-it-right kind of guy, the kind of guy you hoped would become a judge, and he did. His opinions were well written but more important than that, he just had an empathy for people who came to his court. He treated the lawyers right, and anyone else in his court."

Meierhenry, who died in July 2020, had a reputation for taking tough cases that other attorneys wouldn't touch, according to his law partner, Clint Sargent.[32]

"Somebody would come in with a new case and they'd pitch him on it and it would be something that maybe three other lawyers turned down because it was too hard, or it was too novel, and Mark's common line was, 'Oh, this is going to be fun!'" Sargent said.

That concern about making sure everyone had access to legal counsel was evident early in Meierhenry's career. After he graduated from the University of South Dakota School of Law, he took a position as a legal aid attorney and later became director of South Dakota Legal Services for the Crow Creek, Lower Brule and Rosebud Indian Reservations from 1970 to 1974.

"Mark started his career in legal aid working with my father [Bill Janklow] and ended up running the program all over South Dakota and he never lost his zeal for helping the little guy," said Russ Janklow.

"He was regarded as one of the foremost experts in our state's history on Indian jurisdiction issues. He was also universally regarded as one of the top jury trial lawyers in the state's history and a mentor to many of us in the profession, just a true class act," Janklow said.[33]

Attorney General Mark Meierhenry. *Courtesy of the Meierhenry family.*

Meierhenry's road to law contained some twists and turns. Born in Gregory in 1944 two weeks after his father was killed in World War II, he moved with his widowed mother to live with her parents. He took his undergraduate degree at USD in 1966 and his law degree in 1970, four years after the graduation of Rick Johnson and two other well-known classmates, William Janklow and James Abourezk, who became a U.S. senator.

Meierhenry was encouraged to run for attorney general by Janklow, and he served two terms before returning to private practice in 1987.

As the trial neared its opening in April 1982, Janklow said this about Meierhenry: "One should never underestimate Mark Meierhenry. He's a good lawyer, a good researcher and as good a prosecutor as anybody I know."[34]

Then, invoking a football simile, the governor continued: "He's like Joe Namath—he calls great plays and he makes great passes; he's calm, easy-going and never outwardly shows any scrambling. This case will be decided by the facts and not the skill of the lawyers because they are evenly matched."[35]

That opinion was shared by John Blackburn, a Yankton trial attorney who knew Meierhenry well. "Mark was a leader and he would work. Would I let him defend me or take a case for me? Yes. There are legions of attorneys in South Dakota I would not because they have not tried anything."

Blackburn said Meierhenry's ability to paint an oral picture in the courtroom was one of his strongest assets. "He was a great storyteller. He would hold forth."

And then there was the side of Meierhenry not normally seen that Davison County coroner George Bittner observed at trial. Bittner and another witness were being briefed by Meierhenry prior to their testimony. "Before I testified," Bittner said, "I was in the room with Kim Tatum and I was impressed with Mark Meierhenry's professionalism. He was preparing us for testimony and the process. He gave us a degree of comfort. He was gentle with Kim Tatum. How he prepared her for the testimony—not suggesting what she should or should not say—but putting her at ease before she testified."

Meierhenry's friend Dave Volk, who coauthored several children's books with Meierhenry, recalled that later in his career he became a nationwide expert in condemnation cases and won a number of cases against the State of South Dakota.

"I think the awards and honors he received from his fellow attorneys tell you all you need to know of what an incredible lawyer he was."

Volk watched Meierhenry in court during the Mathis trial. "He was excellent and today would have gotten a conviction. People back then just could not believe that a father could murder his family."

Meierhenry's deputy prosecutor for the state, Dennis Holmes, had been in the attorney general's office for less than three years when the Mathis murders occurred but already was head of the litigation unit. A Custer native, Holmes graduated from the USD School of Law in May 1979, as did his boss before him.

"Meierhenry was just such a great mentor," Holmes remembers. "You were too young to know you were in over your head. He was the greatest mentor anyone could have had. He gave you an assignment, helped you on the way."

Holmes was busy early, taking on Indian jurisdictional issues and advising the state highway patrol on legal matters. He rose to deputy attorney general and chief deputy attorney general before moving on to the U.S. Attorney's Office in 1988.

The Mathis case "was essentially Mark's case," Holmes recalls. "He would tell you what he wanted you to do. I tried several cases with Mark. You were the No. 2 and he was in charge. You needed to be ready to do almost anything."

The two men split up many of the witnesses during the Mathis trial, and sometimes there were surprises.

"Mark would change his mind. He was a big idea man. I said at Mark's passing that I don't think I was ever involved with a person who could think on his feet faster than Mark."

Holmes started with the U.S. Attorney's Office in Pierre, then transferred in 1995 to the Sioux Falls office, where he served in numerous roles. He was lead attorney in the Organized Crime and Drug Enforcement Task Force, senior litigation counsel and criminal chief. He was acting U.S. attorney on two occasions.

It wasn't just Meierhenry who had confidence in Holmes. After he moved to the U.S. Attorney's Office, one of his bosses over the years was former U.S. attorney Marty Jackley, who described Holmes this way: "I can tell you this. He's always extremely well prepared. He has a strong courtroom demeanor.

"He always handled the hard cases. Not just hard proof cases but hard emotion cases. He's been the go-to guy to handle those big, high-profile cases in South Dakota. He's never sought glory or fame from it. He just goes in and does his job," Jackley said.

One of those high-profile cases was the Debra Jenner murder trial, successfully prosecuted by Holmes. In 1987, Jenner, a Huron woman, was accused of stabbing her three-year-old daughter more than seventy times with a knife and toy metal airplane. It was one of South Dakota's most horrific crimes.

Holmes was Jackley's first assistant and criminal chief, and when Jackley left the office and Brendan Johnson was appointed, there was a gap, filled by Holmes. "Dennis on my recommendation acted as U.S. attorney," Jackley said.

Another former U.S. attorney, Randy Seiler, said one of Holmes's many skills was his ability to connect with juries. "Dennis was so matter-of-fact and dependable that juries have a level of confidence in him based on his approach. He has an uncanny way of connecting with juries. He's not flamboyant, but he thoroughly and accurately presents the facts."

As of 2020, Holmes was continuing his work in the U.S. Attorney's Office.

Chapter 6
TRIAL BEGINS

Seven months after Ladonna Mathis and her two of her sons were shot in their sleep, all eyes in South Dakota turned to Yankton, where the twice-postponed trial would begin Monday, April 12, 1982.

Ladonna's husband, John Mathis, had pleaded not guilty to three counts of first-degree murder, indictments handed down by a grand jury in Mitchell on October 30.

Judge Thomas Anderst and attorneys for the state and defense convened in chambers to dispose of housekeeping matters, including a seven-page questionnaire developed by the judge with input from the attorneys. The questionnaire contained biographical information and asked if the prospective juror had any connection to the Mathis family. It also asked if the prospective juror had ever been the victim of a crime and if he or she knew any members of law enforcement in Yankton County. Defense attorney Johnson criticized the questionnaire as a "watered down, compromise version."[36]

Before jury selection began, Anderst disposed of more motions from both sides, denying a defense motion to dismiss the case because of a news story in the Sioux Falls *Argus Leader*. Defense attorney Johnson argued that comments by Meierhenry and his support of the death penalty were prejudicial to the case.

"Attorney General Meierhenry believes the defendant is his best witness. Now the attorney general knows well that the defendant doesn't have to offer any testimony in this case. This statement is prejudicial," Johnson insisted.[37]

Left: The Yankton Public Safety Center, where the 1982 trial of John Mathis was held. *Courtesy of James L. Van Osdel.*

Right: Judge Thomas Anderst. *Courtesy of the Anderst family.*

Meierhenry countered, saying he only agreed to the interview in question after learning that the defense counsel and defendant had already been interviewed by the same reporter.[38]

Johnson also objected to the jury selection process, saying that too many prospective jurors were dismissed because of their occupation, including physicians, dentists, nurses and sole proprietors. He asked the judge to install a new panel of potential jurors to ensure a fair trial. Anderst also denied that motion, saying fair jurors could be selected and that a good cross-section of the community could be achieved.[39]

The judge granted each side the right to blackball three additional jurors, which gave both the defense and prosecution twenty-three such disqualifications.[40]

The Yankton Public Safety Center, built in 1975 to replace the historic 1905 county courthouse, housed three courtrooms on the second floor. The largest, Courtroom A, contained room for approximately one hundred persons. The first two rows were reserved for press and photographers, and the balance of the space was used for prospective jurors. Fifty of the 150 prospective jurors reported on the second day and were assigned a number, as attorneys began a process expected to last up to a week.

Horror in the Heartland

Though the 1905 Yankton County Courthouse was historic and beautiful, the Yankton County Public Safety Center was used for the John Mathis murder trial because of its modern courtrooms and an elevator. The trial was moved there on a change of venue from Davison County. The picturesque courthouse was later deemed unsafe and demolished in 2003. *Public domain.*

During questioning, Johnson focused on how each prospect would vote in the case if a vote was called on that day. He delved into each prospect's attitude regarding life insurance, media coverage, hunting, drug use and Attorney General Meierhenry's involvement in the case, as well as their ability to look at gruesome photographs. He also asked about any connection any of the prospects had with anyone involved in the case.[41]

Meierhenry's questioning turned to the death penalty when he asked a prospective juror how she felt about it. When she said she opposed it, Meierhenry twice challenged her for cause, but both times, Anderst overruled him, prompting a meeting in chambers with the judge and defense counsel.

A challenge for cause is a request by an attorney that a prospective juror be dismissed because the attorney has a specific reason to believe that the person cannot be impartial when serving as a juror. It differs from a peremptory challenge, which an attorney may use without stating any reason.

Following the conference, Meierhenry continued to ask prospective jurors about their attitude toward the death penalty, but they were not automatically discharged if they opposed it.[42]

Anderst, while not issuing a gag order on jurors, told them they shouldn't discuss the case with anyone or among themselves. He advised them that they were to make their judgments based on what they heard in court and not to watch or read news accounts of the trial.

The process was slow going. Only six jurors were questioned in the Tuesday morning session and nine in the afternoon. When court adjourned, five had been excused and ten remained. Fifteen jurors were needed for the trial—twelve to be seated and three as alternates.

Even though Meierhenry and Johnson grew up in the same town and had been friends for years, they still exhibited some testiness during the selection of jurors. When questioning Glen L. Gross, Johnson said: "This is a very serious case—probably the most serious case that has ever happened in the state of South Dakota."

Meierhenry objected, saying Johnson was making a statement instead of asking a question. Anderst sustained the objection. When Meierhenry was questioning Gross, he asked him if he could be objective. "You won't let sympathy for the defendant or smooth-talking lawyers sway you, then?"

Johnson objected, which was also sustained.[43]

After court recessed on Wednesday, Meierhenry waxed philosophical.

"The whole jury process sometimes defies common sense," he said. "You've got lawyers asking convoluted questions that they word in legal terminology that's basically for the benefit of the appellate court. The appellate courts hem us in and make it not very creative to be in the law business because everybody's afraid of being reversed."[44] The defense team repeatedly asked prospective jurors if they had ever known someone who sank into a deep depression after the loss of a loved one. They probed jurors one by one about any prejudgments they might have made about Mathis. And they repeated a question that cast doubts on John Mathis's intellectual capacity. "You wouldn't hold it against him that he's not an articulate or a particularly bright person?" Johnson asked Ray L. Harris.[45]

Meierhenry focused on whether jurors would consider imposing the death penalty, which he said he would request if Mathis was convicted. Two potential jurors, a Roman Catholic nun and a United Church of Christ lay minister, said they could not consider capital punishment under any circumstances.

Interestingly, Johnson and Eklund provided a list of 370 potential jurors to the state.[46] After three days of jury selection, sixty-three Yankton County residents had been questioned. Eight women and six men were retained for further examination as the process moved into its fourth day and appeared to be headed for the following week.

The media coverage of the state's most sensational trial since Jack McCall was tried in Yankton in 1876 was the talk of the town. Cliff Hanson, retired, said he had faith in Yankton people to serve as jurors with integrity. "I think this guy's going to get a fair trial in Yankton if he can get it anywhere," Hanson said. "You know, I feel sorry for that guy—every time I see him on TV. He's not guilty yet and only the court can prove him guilty. The loudmouths and dumbbells, they're all alike and they're always the same, but it's not for me and it's not for them to sit in the coffeeshops and judge."[47]

On Monday, April 19, the selection of twelve jurors and three alternates was completed late in the afternoon after four days of painstaking questioning by attorneys. Six men and six women made up the jury, which would decide the fate of John Mathis, accused of killing his wife and two sons. The youngest juror was twenty-seven; the oldest, sixty-nine. All were white and almost all lived in Yankton.

The jurors were Lynette Hansen, bookkeeper at Hansen Floor and Paint; Ray L. Harris, manager of a shoe store; Deanna P. Erickson, grocery clerk at Sav-U-More; Burnell Haugen, electrical worker; Barbara Bosch, tutor; Jane Ludens King, special education teacher; Edward Kellar, electrician with Dale Electronics; Gary Honomichl, owner of the Butcher Block Restaurant; Patricia Holmes, food service employee with the Yankton School system; Dennis Kralicek, welder at Kolberg Manufacturing; Teressa Beavers, of Gayville, a clerk at Northwest Public Service utility company; and Elmer Hauck, retired employee of the Human Services Center. The three alternates were Elaine Harty, Shirley Kokesh and David Hack.[48]

With the jury seated at last, Meierhenry stated his case firmly and succinctly. "The right man is on trial, the right man is accused. Mathis is guilty," he told jurors.

Then, for the better part of an hour, he outlined what the prosecution would show, using early testimony by John Mathis, the questioning of Mathis by law enforcement officers and laboratory reports from the FBI. Meierhenry also said he would show that Mathis lied to law enforcement officers and, further, that the gunshot wound to Mathis's left arm was self-inflicted. Moreover, he said, the state would show that Mathis had a relationship with a neighbor girl who was the family's babysitter and that the relationship was at first a secret from Mathis's wife, Ladonna. "There was sexual contact between he and the young girl," Meierhenry said. The

Attorney general and prosecutor Mark Meierhenry answers questions from reporters. *Courtesy of the* Daily Republic.

young girl, Kim Tatum, seventeen, told her mother, Bonnie Tatum, who told Mathis to stay away from her daughter.[49]

The defense used only fifteen minutes in its opening statement. Wally Eklund told jurors that Mathis had been "tested psychiatrically and psychologically. There's no way with his amount of intelligence he could have constructed and carried out this type of crime." He said testimony would show that Mathis had a difficult time in school. Eklund ridiculed the state's investigation and said evidence would show it "was not directed to finding more evidence but an attempt to play on John's mind." Eklund said that contrary to the state's statement, there was no sexual contact between Mathis and the neighbor girl, Kim Tatum. Eklund said the defense intended to show that the state failed to concentrate on any other suspects in the case and failed to check "a drug burnout two or three miles away."[50]

In addition to its opening statements, the state called a parade of witnesses, including Dawn Tatum, fourteen, Kim's younger sister, who was apparently the last person to see Ladonna Mathis and her two sons alive, about 8:45 the night before the shootings. Also called were Davison County deputy sheriff Kirkus, who responded first to the call from John Mathis to the site of the murders; Raymond Judy from Woonsocket, who testified to the phone calls made from the Mathis telephone in the machine shed; Marlin Shriver and Stan Loon, livestock truck drivers from Letcher, who said they saw no one on the area roads the night of the murders; and George Bittner, Davison County coroner, who testified to the color photographs of the deceased taken at the scene.[51]

Meierhenry read the grand jury indictment charging Mathis with the murder of his wife and two sons on September 8 on the family farm eight miles north and one mile east of Mount Vernon. According to the indictment, Mathis shot his wife and sons as they lay sleeping in their beds in the machine shed that was their temporary home while a new home was being completed. A suspicious basement fire had damaged the Mathis home on July 9, according to deputy fire marshal Pat Harrington, and then the home was destroyed by fire after a lightning strike on July 22. About 2:30 a.m. on September 8, Meierhenry said, Mathis used a Marlin .22-caliber semiautomatic rifle to shoot his wife twice in the head. One of those wounds was fatal.[52] Then, Meierhenry told the attentive audience in Courtroom A, Mathis shot his two-year-old son, Patrick, clad in blue sleeper pajamas, once in the back of the head, with the bullet exiting the skull through an eye. Then Mathis shot Brian, four, in the ear; the wound was immediately fatal. "Evidently Patrick was not dead," Meierhenry said. "He got up and turned around and was shot again from the front, into the eye, and the bullet came out the back of the head. This shot killed him."[53] Meierhenry said most of the shots were fired at close range, but the last and lethal shot fired into Patrick came from farther away.[54]

In his opening statement, Eklund told the jury that his client encountered the intruder as he was leaving the machine shed. Mathis was returning from checking on some farrowing hogs. Mathis contended he was shot on the inside of the left forearm while scuffling with the intruder. After lying unconscious for several minutes, he awoke and found his wife and sons killed in their beds. He called Deputy Sheriff Kirkus, a former Mount Vernon High School classmate, for help.[55]

Meierhenry wanted all sixty-one photographs of the crime scene made available to the jury, but Judge Anderst threw out twenty-two of them because they were too gruesome to show to a jury. The photos, mostly close-ups of the murdered family, were objected to by Mathis attorney Rick Johnson. "The pictures were gruesome since the victims were uncovered and do not portray the condition they were found in," Johnson said, adding they would "do nothing except make some people sick or in some cases prejudice some people by the sight of them."[56]

Meierhenry also told the court that the .22-caliber rifle shell found in Mathis's pocket after his clothes were removed at a Mitchell hospital the morning of the shooting would loom large as a significant part of the trial. Meierhenry said Mathis told authorities that Patrick found the live .22 shell in the yard and was seen playing with it the night before the shooting. Mathis told authorities he questioned his son about the shell, took it from the boy and put it in his pocket.[57]

Meierhenry admitted he did not have evidence to answer all the questions raised by his basically circumstantial case. "This is not like Perry Mason or Quincy. We don't have a script writer to fill in the blanks," he said. Eklund, meanwhile, said Meierhenry's case was riddled with blank spots, ineptly investigated and misconstrued by the state, which Eklund said didn't even bother to search for the real killer.

"The whole investigation was an attempt to play on John's mind or an attempted play to get him to confess or admit to a crime he didn't do," Eklund said. He also said there was hard evidence to clear his client. A test of Mathis's hand to see if he had fired a gun came out negative, and no gold spray paint was found on his hands or clothes.[58]

Chapter 7

PROSECUTION PRESSES AHEAD

The state introduced its strongest testimony to date on Wednesday, April 21, when Deputy Sheriff Kirkus began what would be three days detailing what he saw at the murder scene. Before he took the stand, however, jurors were shown a ten-minute videotape filmed about seven thirty the morning of the slayings. The tape showed the bodies of the victims, scenes from the outside the shed, the front door, the area where Mathis said he wrestled with a masked man and pieces of evidence, such as rifle shells and a green cap found in the area of the alleged attack on Mathis.[59]

The courtroom, packed and generally noisy with whispering, coughing and notebook-flipping spectators, became silent as jurors looked at the victims.[60]

Kirkus was the first to arrive on the scene early in the morning of September 8, after receiving a call from John Mathis at 3:54 a.m. Much of his testimony focused on the absence of blood in the area where Mathis said he struggled with a masked assailant, who he said shot him in the left forearm. Mathis said he blacked out for thirty or forty-five minutes after the scuffle. But Kirkus testified there were no footprints, car tracks, or blood anywhere in that area. In short, Mathis's story about his struggle with a mysterious masked man "didn't wash" and led Kirkus to suspect him in the shooting deaths of his family.[61]

Kirkus said the only blood found was inside the machine shed where bodies were discovered. Kirkus also contradicted another key part of the Mathis version of the morning's events. Mathis said when he regained consciousness, he crawled to the machine shed door and "looked across the room and could see blood" and that's when he called Kirkus. But Kirkus testified that there was no way someone entering the machine shop could have seen the beds or the condition of the victims in them. The beds were at the far end of the building, and "when you enter the machine shed you could maybe at best see the outline of John's bed, but any farther, you couldn't see," Kirkus testified.

Eklund and Johnson cross-examined Kirkus aggressively for two hours, with Eklund asking Kirkus, "Didn't you tell him his story just wouldn't wash?" To which Kirkus replied, "I believe I did." In an attempt to paint a picture of a slipshod investigation, in which Kirkus and others jumped to the conclusion that Mathis had committed the murders, Eklund asked Kirkus if he had suggested to Mathis during the interrogation that he might have been mentally ill and killed his wife and two sons. Kirkus said no, nor had he insinuated that because Mathis's mother was mentally ill, he might have problems as well.[62]

A bloodstained pillow was one of many gruesome items taken into evidence following the September 8 murders of Ladonna Mathis and two of her sons. *Courtesy of the Davison County Sheriff's Department.*

"Are the words 'just doesn't wash' part of your training?" Eklund asked Kirkus. Then Eklund probed an area that the defense believed showed an investigatory lapse. Kirkus acknowledged that no fingerprints were taken anywhere on the farm, but he had told Meierhenry in direct testimony that so many people had come and gone at the scene that taking fingerprints seemed futile. Eklund also asked if anyone had thought to check whether the engines in any of the Mathis vehicles were warm. If a warm engine had been found, it could have suggested that a vehicle had been driven to dispose of the murder weapon.

An exchange between Eklund and Kirkus revealed the defense's strategy: "Who was involved in checking around the farm?" Eklund asked.

"I believe DCI Agent (Bernie) Christenson, Sheriff (Lyle) Swenson, possibly Deputy (Don) Radel and I'm not sure who else," Kirkus replied.

"You mean with all those law enforcement officers around, nobody thought to check those engines and see if they were warm?" Eklund asked.

"That is correct," Kirkus answered.[63]

Kirkus also disputed Eklund's suggestion that Mathis's physical appearance indicated he'd been in a fight. Referring to the wound in Mathis's left arm and his appearance, Eklund asked, "That's not conclusive of a fight?" Answered Kirkus, "Not necessarily."

Earlier, Dr. Walter Baas, the Mathis family physician, testified that he had attended to Mathis's gunshot wound, which was in the thumb side of the upper left forearm, and an exit wound below on the little finger side of the forearm. When Meierhenry asked Baas if Mathis's wound was consistent with a self-inflicted gunshot wound, defense attorney Johnson objected but was overruled. Baas said the gunshot wound, as well as abrasions on the knuckles of Mathis's right hand, a cut inside his upper lip and a small circular red mark on his upper right cheek, could have been "potentially self-inflicted." But Johnson challenged Baas's testimony by objecting loudly, "You can't self-inflict a bullet wound without a gun, can you doctor?" reminding jurors and others in the courtroom that no murder weapon had been found.[64]

Bernie Christenson, assistant director of the state Division of Criminal Investigation when the murders occurred, was among those on the farm scene early. He later served in the state legislature and helped Governor George Mickelson launch the South Dakota Community Foundation. *Courtesy of the South Dakota Community Foundation.*

Other witnesses for the state also testified, including Donna Wieczorek, a nurse at Methodist Hospital, where Mathis was taken by ambulance the morning of the murders. Wieczorek testified that she detected no manure or odor from Mathis's boots, even though Mathis said he had gone to two hog barns before returning and encountering the masked man with whom he struggled. "Are you telling this jury Mathis couldn't have been in the hog barn?" defense attorney Johnson asked her. Wieczorek replied that she "didn't detect any unusual odor."[65]

Sheriff Swenson testified that at no time in his initial investigation did he find any evidence of an intruder on the Mathis farm. Asked by prosecutor

Attorney General Mark Meierhenry shows the jury a drawing of what defendant John Mathis described as a "hooded, masked man" who killed his family. *Dave Fuller drawing, Lyle Swenson collection.*

Meierhenry if he detected any evidence that led him to believe a masked intruder was on the farm, Swenson said, "Absolutely none." He said he and other authorities checked for tire tracks and footprints and inspected the surrounding area, including the machine shed, for any evidence. A sixth spent cartridge was discovered when he and two other officers were standing on the cement apron of the shed.[66]

Bullets from a .22-caliber rifle were a central part of the case from the early hours of the investigation. As DCI agent David Muller explained, using a drawing on a large whiteboard, five spent cartridges were found in the shed near the victims. One was found against the northwest wall behind Brian's bed. A second was between the beds of Ladonna Mathis and her husband. A third was under the foot of Ladonna's bed. A fourth was between the beds of Patrick and Brian and a fifth between the northwest wall and Ladonna's bed. The sixth cartridge was discovered outside the shop when a glint of sunlight shone upon it.[67]

The bullet found by DCI agent Ken Giegling in John Mathis's pants pocket at the hospital on the morning of the murders was also a .22 caliber, the same as the spent cartridges found at the murder scene. But was it from the same source? Defense attorneys would contend throughout the trial that .22-caliber shells are common on farms across South Dakota. Most farmers and ranchers own a .22 rifle and use it to keep varmints at bay. But prosecutors had been unable to find a .22 rifle on John Mathis's farm. The only gun discovered on the Mathis farm was an older model .243 rifle that Mathis himself had pointed out to Kirkus the morning of the slayings. Investigators confiscated at least six .22 rifles for examination, including rifles owned by Vern Mathis, John Mathis's father; Dan Pollard, boyfriend of Kim Tatum, the Mathis babysitter; and neighbor Robert Fortner. None was a match for the shells found at the scene.

Nevertheless, the victims were killed with a .22-caliber rifle. The spent casings were found at the scene. John Mathis had an unspent .22 in his pants pocket. Giegling testified that Mathis did not tell him about the bullet when he interviewed Mathis at the hospital.[68]

Giegling said he had not read Mathis his Miranda rights at the hospital because he was not a suspect at the time. He said Mathis gave his approval when he was asked if his clothing could be used for chemical tests to determine if gun grease, solvent from gun-cleaning solutions or shaving cream used by the assailant could have been left on his clothes. The tests, according to Giegling, came up negative. Giegling added that the primary test destroyed the evidence and negated any further tests of the hand swab evidence.[69] But on redirect examination, Meierhenry asked, "If someone's wearing gloves, those chemicals don't generally go through gloves, do they?" Giegling agreed.[70]

The state continued its efforts to discredit John Mathis's "masked man" story. If there was such an intruder and he escaped, wouldn't there be a fear that he would return and, if so, what safety precautions had been taken at

Attorney General Mark Meierhenry (*left*) and DCI agent Ken Giegling discuss the grand jury investigation of the death of Ladonna Mathis with law enforcement officials. Giegling had presented what Meierhenry described as "electrifying evidence." *Courtesy of the* Daily Republic.

the farm, prosecutor Meierhenry wondered. In part of his hour-and-ten-minute examination, Vern Mathis Sr. said the only thing his son had done as a protective measure was to "stay alert" to any outside threats. Meierhenry asked the elder Mathis: Had he armed himself? Were deadbolt locks installed on the door? Special alarms on the windows? No, Mathis said; none of these measures had been taken.

Meierhenry then turned to potential enemies of the Mathis family who could be suspects in the killings. The defense had maintained all along that the state had short-circuited good investigative procedure when it focused on John Mathis as the prime and, somewhat later, as the only suspect in the case. But the state disputed that argument, saying it had looked at other potential suspects, but nothing materialized. One of those persons of interest was Greg Borman, who had sold fuel not only to John Mathis but also to other family members. All five had stopped doing business with Borman, but the elder Mathis, who admitted to discussing Borman with Sheriff Swenson, testified that he could recall no argument or confrontation with Borman as a result of the business termination.[71]

The following day, Tuesday, April 27, forensic pathologist Dr. Brad Randall of Sioux Falls testified that Patrick Mathis, two, was likely awake when he was shot. Randall told the jury that Patrick was shot in the back of the neck, but that wound was not fatal. "Patrick was alive with a beating heart after he sustained an injury to his muscle," Randall said. The second wound, which struck Patrick in the left eye and exited from the bottom of the neck, was the fatal wound. "At some point later," after the first shot, "he either sat up or kneeled in bed. At that point he sustained the second wound," Randall testified.[72] He said Patrick was lying on his stomach when the first shot was fired, but his body was found on its back. Two separate pools of blood were also found in Patrick's bed. Photos showing the position of the victim were shown to the jury, over the defense's objections. The older son, Brian, four, died instantly, Randall testified, from a wound in the right ear. The jury also saw a slide of Ladonna Mathis's head, punctured by bullet wounds in the temple and the neck. Mathis looked away from the screen and held his arm over his face.[73]

Randall, in a February 2021 interview, said that to the best of his recollection there was no way to determine if the fatal gunshot wound to Ladonna Mathis was the first or second shot fired. The gunshot wound near her left ear was the lethal wound, according to the autopsy report. A second gunshot wound in the left neck did not appear to involve any vital structures.

However, when it came to Patrick, who also was shot twice, Randall was able to ascertain that the first shot to the back neck region passed through the soft tissue of the head, exiting lateral to the left eye. "It appeared to be a non-lethal wound," Randall's report said. The second wound to the face extended downward through the nasal sinuses and severed the spinal cord. "The second wound was sufficiently severe to represent a near instantaneous cause of death. It is impossible to estimate the time which may have elapsed between the first and second gunshot wound. The decedent could conceivably have lived for at least several minutes after the first gunshot wound was inflicted," Randall wrote.

Dr. Brad Randall, a Sioux Falls forensic pathologist, testified that Patrick Mathis, two, was shot twice by the assailant because the first shot failed to kill him. *Courtesy of Brad Randall.*

Matching the bullet recovered behind the bed where Patrick was sleeping to the other bullet strongly suggested that Patrick sat up after the first shot, since he would have been unable to sit up had he received the lethal wound first. In Ladonna Mathis's case, no position change between the two shots was evident, and so it was not possible to determine which shot was fired first, Randall said. She could have been killed instantly by the first shot, and the perpetrator fired a second shot to be certain. Or, in a rapid-fire sequence, the victim did not have time to move between the first and second shots.

The jury was also called to absorb lengthy evidence testimony on bullets, and FBI agent John Dillon Jr. testified that gunpowder particles found on Mathis's shirt were "consistent with shooting a weapon." FBI agent Richard Reem testified that blood enzyme samples taken from Mathis, a shirt he had wrapped around his wounded arm, and a dried pool of blood on the machine shed floor were likewise consistent with Mathis's type A blood. The blood sample from between Ladonna Mathis's and Patrick's beds was not from either of the victims, and Meierhenry was expected to contend that it was from Mathis as a result of a self-inflicted wound.[74]

Defense attorneys Eklund and Johnson challenged the blood tests' validity, pointing out that the state had admitted that the first test sample sent to the FBI lab was not Mathis's, which necessitated a second sample be taken from Mathis while Kirkus and Eklund were witnesses. The defense contended that the blood testing procedure, like the overall investigation, was error-ridden and inept.[75]

Prosecution witness Ernest Peele, FBI agent in the elemental analysis unit in Washington, D.C., testified that the bullet fragments recovered at the crime scene and spent bullets and fragments recovered from the murder victims were all generally similar to a Winchester Super X bullet recovered from Mathis's pants pocket in the hospital.[76] A sixth bullet had some differences, but Peele said he could not rule out that it came from the same box. Under cross-examination, Peele admitted that the bullets found at the scene had twice as much copper as the bullet found in Mathis's pocket.[77] At the same time, Elya Zeldes, state crime laboratory supervisor, said the six cartridges found at the scene were all fired from the same gun. He concluded that the rifle was a semi-automatic .22 caliber, likely made by Marlin. He also told the jury that the bullet found in Mathis's pocket did not appear to have been lying outside. Mathis had testified to the grand jury—and that testimony was entered into the trial court record—that his son Patrick had found the bullet, probably outside on the ground.[78]

Chapter 8

A MATTER OF MOTIVE

From the very beginning, the state's case had three fundamental challenges: No murder weapon, no witnesses, and no strong motive.

Although law enforcement believed that there was no "masked man" and John Mathis had cold-bloodedly killed his wife and two of his sons, the .22-caliber rifle murder weapon eluded a thorough and painstaking search that took weeks to complete. Part of the challenge was the sheer size of the crime scene. The Mathis farm contained nine buildings, any of which could have been used to hide the rifle.

Investigators were well aware of the challenge and even stated that the only way to know for certain if the weapon was still on site would be to tear down each building stick by stick and board by board. They decided such an approach was not feasible. Which wasn't to say that law enforcement officials cut corners in their efforts to locate the gun. They scoured the land around the buildings for miles, walking nearly shoulder to shoulder through fields, watching for anything that seemed out of place or unusual. They rode on horseback through roadside ditches. They used metal detectors, without result.

The Secret Witness phone line provided a number of ideas for law enforcement, if not concrete leads. One Sioux Falls woman wondered if the gun "had been dropped down between the studs in the walls from the attic at the house. I understand that it was a new house and I don't know whether that is possible. Good luck on the case." Another person told the searchers to "look down the chimney of the new house for the gun in the Mattis [sic] murder."[79]

South Dakota's Mathis Murders

Despite the grimness of the ordeal, one search effort produced a humorous effect in the context of human tragedy.

Dennis Kaemingk, a detective with the Mitchell Police Department, spent two or three days at the crime scene helping the Davison County Sheriff's Office and the state DCI. Mutual aid among law enforcement agencies was common, and even off-duty officials assisted in the comprehensive search of the fields and buildings.

"The only field I helped search was just south of the farm, across the road," Kaemingk said in a 2020 interview. "I remember being out there, a cornfield if I remember. We walked six or seven feet apart, looking for anything that wasn't normal. Anything that was out of place.

"We even thought maybe he had taken a fence post out, and dug down, and put the post on top of it. We jiggled fence posts. I remember searching through the outbuildings, grassy areas, shelterbelts. We looked through everything but we hadn't checked the hog confinement and the pit."

The pit was the large collection tank directly below the hog barn. A common practice for confinement hog raising was to have the animals on slatted floors, so waste products would flow directly below to a pit or lagoon.

Two days after the murders, law enforcement officials continued their search for the murder weapon at the John Mathis farm, excavating animal waste tanks. *Courtesy of the* Daily Republic.

When the pit was filled, it was pumped out, and the waste material was sometimes spread as fertilizer on the property owner's farmland.

Sheriff Swenson and others thought perhaps the murder weapon had been thrown into the pit. Kaemingk and Bernie Christenson, assistant director of the DCI, volunteered to search the lagoon. First, Kaemingk remembered, it had to be pumped down to a level of about four feet so he and Christenson could walk in it.

"I remember the conversation that everything was going to cost a lot of money. They said we need to search but we needed a pump first. They got a pump to pump it down.

"When you walk in the door of the building there is a ladder down to the pit. We stood there looking at the pit and looked at the walls and immediate area to see if there was anything unusual. The pigs were still up top. They had not emptied the building."

Using oxygen tanks, breathing apparatus, and hats provided by the fire department, Kaemingk and Christenson descended into the pit. Both were tied to a rope to rescue them if they got into trouble. Dressed in waders, they crisscrossed the lagoon, up to their armpits in animal sewage.

"We were down there I don't how long. I was on east side and Bernie was on the west side closest to the door and the breathing apparatus had alarms on them that sounded like a bell to tell you when air was low. Bernie is bigger and he used more air and his alarm went off and all the pigs ran to the east side and unloaded on me. On my hat, inside my wet suit, and I'm thinking what a glamourous job I have."

The search produced nothing. The men climbed out and local firefighters hosed them down.

But the odor remained, Kaemingk recalled. "The stink sticks to you, clings to you. I was home in the tub and Wyonne [his wife] brought jars of tomato juice and I took a bath in tomato juice. That helped a lot."

The prosecution developed theories about what had happened to the rifle and tested several guns that they thought might have been connected to the cases. All the tests turned up negative. The lack of a murder weapon was used more than once by the defense team in its efforts to show the jury that John Mathis did not shoot his wife and sons. The murder weapon, Mathis's lawyers contended, was kept by the masked intruder, who took it with him when he fled.

Just as challenging to the prosecution was defining a motive for its only suspect, John Mathis. What would cause a man to kill his own wife and children? What incentive would be so powerful? The state decided early that it was not money, for the insurance policy of $60,000 on Ladonna Mathis seemed insufficient to justify such an act.

Two days after the murder, Deputy Kirkus and DCI agent Lorin Pankratz interviewed the Mathis family babysitter, Kim Tatum, whose family lived across the highway to the west. A cheerleader and honor student, the seventeen-year-old Tatum confirmed that Mathis had tried to kiss her when they were alone. She thought the first time Mathis kissed her would have been sometime in 1979. She had been babysitting, and when he paid her, he gave her a quick kiss. He kissed her again in the spring of 1981 when they were working in the hog barn.[80] Tatum told the deputies that Mathis had tried to put his hands on her breasts; she told him that it was wrong, and he said that he knew it was wrong and apologized. She did not recall Mathis telling her he loved her, but he did say that he liked her a great deal. On one occasion, Mathis told her that he wished he hadn't gotten married and he wished he had met her first.

In a followup interview by Kirkus and DCI agent Giegling two days later, Tatum admitted to having feelings for Mathis and agreed that Mathis had similar feelings for her. She admitted that Mathis had kissed her, rubbed her breasts and rubbed her between her legs on more than one occasion. Tatum denied ever going to bed with Mathis or having sex with him.

Tatum said that Mathis felt his wife, Ladonna, was the one who wanted to get married when they did.[81]

When the prosecution called Tatum, who had turned eighteen in February, as its first witness on Thursday, April 29, she testified to the kissing and sexual contact and said that when she went to the hospital to visit Mathis after he was wounded in the September 8 shooting incident, he winked at her. On the stand, Tatum was soft-spoken but composed and occasionally looked at Mathis, who looked frequently at the jury. The jurors, on several occasions, were watching Mathis more often than the witness as Tatum told of her relationship with Mathis.[82] Tatum's testimony matched what she had told investigators earlier about the extent of the physical contact: Mathis "touched my breasts and lower parts," she said. Tatum said she protested but admitted that, on a couple occasions, she kissed him back. Mathis had told a grand jury after the murders that he kissed Tatum only once and had no further sexual contact with her. Meierhenry read those grand jury transcripts in the courtroom.[83]

Tatum testified that she and Mathis often talked about her school; her boyfriend, Dan Pollard, to whom she was engaged; and her cheerleading and basketball activities. She said she never told Pollard about the physical

Kim Tatum, the neighbor girl who helped John Mathis with chores, testified about her relationship with Mathis. *Dave Fuller drawing.*

contact. Tatum repeated that Mathis told her he never would have married his wife, had he known Tatum at the time. "He wished he would have met me first," Tatum said.[84]

Tatum also described a time when she was working for Mathis, and he said he wanted to take a nap after dinner. He lay down on his bed, and Tatum rested on the adjacent bed. "I thought there was a fly on me so I brushed it away. But it came back. I looked up and he was sitting there looking at me. I was scared—really scared."

Tatum remembered DCI agent Giegling telling her that "there's no way you can bring little Patrick and little Brian and Ladonna back. There's a 2-year-old boy and a 4-year-old boy and a 31-year-old woman dead and you're worried about your reputation." Tatum said she told defense counsel that she didn't tell everything to the officers who questioned her because she was "embarrassed."[85] On cross-examination, Tatum said officers who questioned her "could have" told her if she didn't cooperate now, she'd "likely be next." Tatum told the officers she didn't believe John Mathis was the kind of man who would kill his wife and family.[86]

When Tatum's mother, Bonnie, testified, she described learning from her daughter three years previously that Mathis had kissed her. "I stopped him and told him to keep his hands off my daughter. I told him if he ever did anything like that again, I was going to tell his wife." Mrs. Tatum was a licensed practical nurse at Methodist Hospital, where Mathis was taken for treatment the morning of the murders. She said she waited with Mathis before he went into surgery. "At one time, I was standing by his bed and he looked up and asked if a person could have two minds."

"I just said no," Mrs. Tatum testified.[87]

In cross-examination by defense attorney Johnson, Kim Tatum made it clear that Mathis never put his hands under her clothes and that they never removed their clothes. "We never had sex, if that's what you're getting at," she said. In a final question, Johnson said, "Miss Tatum, in the final analysis, and I'm not trying to embarrass you; in the final analysis you were never even sexually aroused by any of this, were you?" Tatum replied, "No." But seconds later, Meierhenry, in redirect examination, shot back, "Do you think Mr. Mathis was?" To which Tatum answered, "I don't know, I suppose. He kept on doing it."[88]

While the Tatum testimony clearly captured the courtroom's attention, other testimony offered by the prosecution focused on attempting to undermine Mathis's version of what occurred the morning of the shootings. Walt Miller, a Mitchell jeweler and watchmaker, said he wasn't 1,000 percent sure but felt that the watch Mathis was wearing the morning of the incident had been deliberately destroyed. Miller said the watch looked as though it

State prosecutor Mark Meierhenry discusses trial evidence with Davison County sheriff Lyle Swenson. *Courtesy of the* Daily Republic.

had been intentionally damaged and not from a fall or a gun barrel. Mathis had told investigators that the watch was damaged during his scuffle with the intruder.[89]

Evelyn Gerlach, mother of Ladonna Mathis, testified that Patrick, two, was not potty trained, contrary to statements by John Mathis. She said she never recalled Patrick getting up in the middle of the night and asking to go potty. But during Johnson's cross-examination, Mrs. Gerlach admitted that Patrick had not slept at her home after July 22 when lightning struck the Mathis home, causing a fire that destroyed it.[90]

The testimony of Kim Tatum was the highlight of the prosecution's case and the final day of testimony. Meierhenry and his team produced forty-six witnesses and more than 250 pieces of evidence over nine days.

Meierhenry seemed satisfied with the state's case. "The evidence went in better than I expected," he said. "It's a misconception that we have to lay it all out. Most cases are circumstantial. When you have eyewitnesses, you get a guilty plea—those are the ones you don't try." If you don't have a bloody-fingered, gun-toting defendant, you can fence him in to the point where any other explanation for the crime is unreasonable, he said.

"What's the probability of a little boy finding a shell the night before the murders that experts say came out of the same box? And of all the evidence, why didn't John tell us about the shell?"[91]

Precisely because no smoking gun was found and because there was no evidence of a fight outside the machine shed, Meierhenry said the murders were planned. "The lack of evidence is consistent with the theory that nobody else was there," he said.[92]

After a weekend break, on Monday, May 3, the defense would begin to mount its case.

Chapter 9

PORTRAIT OF A GOOD WOMAN

When Vern Mathis described his daughter-in-law Ladonna as "a little better than the best," no one offered a different opinion.[93] Ladonna was the quintessential farm wife, totally invested in the operation. She helped care for the hogs, loved her children and husband and attended church regularly.

The blue-eyed, five-foot-nine girl with dark brown hair was blessed with straight white teeth and a beautiful smile. She and her three siblings grew up on a farm east of Dimock, before air conditioning and during a time when farm children were expected to help with the family operation.

"Our home life was herding cattle. She knew how to drive a 4010 John Deere as slick as a whistle," remembers her older brother, Dwight Gerlach. "One day when we were baling hay she sheared a pin. She kept those pins and it made me feel a little guilty because every time that happened, I'd get a little upset, and it would make her feel guilty."

It wasn't all work, though, and on some Saturdays Ladonna and her girlfriends would pile into the 1955 green and beige Chevrolet and, with Dwight driving, head to an area dance.

"We would sing songs together because the radio didn't work," Dwight said in a February 2021 interview.

In summer, the family enjoyed going to June Festival in Corsica, which featured a midway carnival and wooden shoe dances. Dwight also took her to Walter League (now called Luther League) and volleyball on Wednesday night. Friday nights usually were reserved for visiting grandparents.

Ladonna started wearing glasses at sixteen, but preferred contacts and obtained some while employed at the National Bank of South Dakota in Corsica.

Dwight recalled one incident that illustrated Ladonna's conscientiousness. "She came home upset. She had made a mistake and counted someone too much money and her till came up short. She didn't know the customer's number and she was walking the floor, worried about that. It was a really, really firm commitment to her job."

Ladonna found out later that two $20 bills had stuck together as she was counting them to the customer.

Ladonna Mathis, age five. *Courtesy of Marilyn Reimnitz.*

Ladonna's younger sister, Marilyn Reimnitz, said in a 2020 interview that the most important things to Ladonna were "her family and her church."

A 1968 graduate of Corsica High School, Ladonna chose not to go to college and instead developed her people skills and learned about business while working at the bank.

"She was very good at sewing and sewed all her own clothes. She raised her own chickens. She was an active member of the Farm Bureau and put together a newsletter," Marilyn recalls. "And she was good at doing hair. She would style her friends' hair."

Ladonna Mathis on her wedding day, May 4, 1973, with her father, Lorenz Gerlach. *Courtesy of Marilyn Reimnitz.*

Ladonna was the business part of the Mathis farm operation, according to Marilyn and others who knew her and her husband. "Maybe John wasn't book smart, but he could do anything with animals. He was excellent at fertilizer application. John could tear a tractor apart and put it back together," Marilyn said, but Ladonna did the books—and sometimes resisted new purchases that John wanted.

Ladonna had told family members on various occasions that items she or the children might want had to be put off many times because the farm operation came first.[94]

"She was able to pay off the farm. Through her knowledge they paid it off. She was very proud of it," Marilyn said.

Who would want to kill her and her children? This was the core question of the murder trial.

In the words of Sheriff Swenson and other investigators, nothing seemed to add up.

Only thirty when she died, a month before her thirty-first birthday, Ladonna was the third of four children born to Lorenz and Evelyn Gerlach. The eldest was Mary Jane; then came Dwight. Marilyn, five years younger than Ladonna, described their relationship as "very close."

Ladonna's ability to plan was apparent outside of the farming operation. She organized her parents' twenty-fifth wedding anniversary, which included a program of singing, guest readings and stories. She repeated the process for their fortieth. For her own wedding reception, Ladonna planned music and stories by family but decided not to have a wedding dance since it would be an added expense, Marilyn said.

Ladonna was active with her youth group at the church, and for her, the most fun was the church plays.

She could also bake and "whip up an apple pie like nothing."

Ladonna liked the song "One Day at a Time," and even though she had no piano at the farm, she bought the sheet music anyway.

"For our parents' 50th anniversary years later, we did sing this song in memory of Ladonna with other guests," Marilyn said.

Ladonna and John dated for two years, so it "wasn't a quick marriage," Marilyn said. "She had a lot of other boys in her life. John was a man that was settled and had something to offer."

Marilyn's future husband, Lyle Reimnitz, and John Mathis were good friends. When John graduated from high school, Lyle invited John and his brother, Vern Jr., to his home because the Mathises did not have a celebration.

Marilyn remembers vividly when Brian and Patrick were living in the machine shed, the Mathises' temporary home after two fires destroyed their house.

Brian was old enough to ride a bike, and "he was thrilled when I rode with him. He would say, 'Would I ride bike with him?'"

Patrick was two, and his mother was trying to potty train him.

Marilyn Reimnitz, younger sister of Ladonna Mathis, in 2021. *Author's collection.*

Horror in the Heartland

The gravestone of Ladonna Mathis and two of her sons in the cemetery north of Mount Vernon. *Courtesy of Doug Kirkus.*

They were happy little guys, little boys with a loving mother, Marilyn said.

Asked what sort of father John was, Marilyn replied, "He didn't spend time with them. He took care of the hogs and fieldwork."

Chapter 10

MATHIS DEFENSE PUSHES BACK

Defense counsel had indicated early on that John Mathis would testify on his own behalf, so when he was called on the first day of the defense's case, it came as no surprise.

Throughout the trial, Wally Eklund and Rick Johnson had based Mathis's defense on these points: Mathis was a hardworking farmer who loved his wife and family; he was not bright enough to have conceived and carried out such a crime; the state did not adequately investigate other possible suspects, nor did it properly gather evidence at the scene; the state and FBI crime labs were guilty of sloppy work on blood samples and bullets; and Mathis's version of what happened at the farm squared with the evidence.

However, before Mathis took the stand, two witnesses were called to bolster the defense's barricade. When asked about an affidavit he signed, in which he described a conversation with a Davison County deputy sheriff, state's attorney Patrick Kiner testified that he could not recall the specific nature of the conversation. In the conversation, Deputy Sheriff Kirkus allegedly noted that Mathis was "hysterical and crying," but Kiner recanted that in his testimony.[95] The second witness, psychologist Thomas Jackson of the University of South Dakota, testified that he administered five tests over six-and-a-half hours, and the results showed that Mathis's "general intellectual functioning was low."

"He was unable to understand complex things and couldn't understand what seems normal," Jackson said. "His abstract reasoning was very bad sometimes although he does very well with his hands."[96]

John Mathis (*center*) is accompanied by his attorneys, Wally Eklund (*left*) and Rick Johnson (*right*). Mathis's brother, Vern Jr. (*far right*), was among those testifying at the trial. *Courtesy of the* Yankton Press & Dakotan.

Meierhenry attempted to discredit the tests by asking Jackson if he had ever been on a farm like Mathis's and Jackson replied he hadn't. "A person running a farm of this size has no problems day in and day out even though he has to make decisions. Is that what you're saying? The farming industry has its problems and you say he is…not good at solving problems?" Meierhenry asked.[97]

When John Mathis took the witness stand, his demeanor was calm and methodical, and he spent the first hour and a half answering questions about his background, family and farming operation. But in the last two hours, when his defense lawyer Eklund asked him about the early morning events of September 8, his pauses were long, his eyes puffy; his voice often quavered when speaking of his wife, Ladonna, and sons Brian and Patrick. Asked directly three separate times if he was guilty, he said "no" each time.[98]

Mathis described the ski-masked intruder as dressed in dark clothing and carrying a long weapon. The assailant was about the same height and build as himself. Then Mathis startled the courtroom when he shouted, "I'll get you, YAAAH," imitating his adversary's threat as he came out of the machine shed. Juror Patricia Holmes threw up her arms, court reporter Gary Lutgen blanched visibly and many of the eighty spectators did a double take.[99]

Mathis testified he reached for the gun, struggled and was shot in the arm before he blacked out. When he woke up, he felt woozy, and his head, teeth and arm hurt as he crawled to the machine shed.

"I tried to wake them up and they wouldn't wake up," he said. He covered up the bodies of his wife and sons, then called Kirkus and his father, Vern Mathis.[100]

Mathis's testimony was summed up in a *Daily Republic* headline: "Mathis recounts same story on witness stand."

Mathis repeated the story he had given to the grand jury. He came home about a quarter after eight in the evening after cutting silage in the cornfield with his father. He and his wife discussed curtains for their new home, which was under construction. He went back outside about nine or a quarter after nine to complete his chores, and returned about ten. His wife and sons were in bed, and he described how he helped his sons through a nightly routine of saying their prayers before tucking them in.[101]

Mathis said he went to bed about ten thirty and was awakened by Patrick, who was standing beside his bed. "I'm not sure if I said something or if I just woke up. I either asked him if, or he repeated, and said he had to go potty." Mathis said he helped the two-year-old to urinate in a pail inside the machine shed.

Mathis then felt that he had to go to the bathroom, so he went into the trees north of the shed. Then, since he was already outside, Mathis said he decided to check the farrowing and finishing barns. When he came out of the barns, where he said exhaust fans and radios are on constantly, he said he heard a vehicle engine idling in the distance to the southwest. When he neared the machine shed, he noticed that a light other than the seven-watt nightlight was on, and he was concerned that one of the youngsters was up and might have wandered out of the building.[102]

As he approached the shed, a masked assailant was coming out, wielding a long gun. They struggled, and the gun went off, wounding Mathis's left arm. Mathis's attorney, Eklund, asked him if he recalled getting hit. "Not really, at the time, no," Mathis said.

Mathis passed out after the gunshot, and when he awakened, he crawled to the shed. When he got inside, he called out for Ladonna, but no one answered. "I could see blood, knew we needed help, found the Mount

Vernon police number and called." His call rang the telephone of Davison County deputy sheriff Kirkus, who lived in Mount Vernon.[103]

On cross-examination, Meierhenry asked Mathis if he had taken any safety precautions after the slayings to protect himself in case the intruder returned. Mathis said he kept a shotgun and shells in the pantry.

"Aren't you afraid of a man out there trying to get you?" Meierhenry asked.

"Let him come. I was just praying he'd come back," Mathis responded.

Meierhenry asked him if he wanted to kill him. Mathis responded, "I'd get him or he'd get me."[104]

Then Meierhenry focused on what the state thought was a key hole in Mathis's story: Why would a masked intruder kill Ladonna Mathis and her two children but leave John Mathis alive?

"Why do you think he didn't shoot you in the head?" Meierhenry asked.

"I don't know," Mathis replied. "I wished he would have."

"Why is that?" Meierhenry asked.

"So that I could be with my family," Mathis said.[105]

In more than three hours of questioning, Meierhenry also pressed Mathis on his relationship with Kim Tatum, which the prosecution saw as the primary motive in the case. Mathis admitted he told his wife he had kissed the babysitter. When Meierhenry asked if it affected his relationship with his

Prosecutor Mark Meierhenry holds a .22-caliber rifle similar to the one used in the murders of Ladonna Mathis and two of her sons. Defendant John Mathis (*far right*) and Judge Thomas Anderst and court reporter Gary Lutgen (*center*) observe. *Dave Fuller drawing, Lyle Swenson collection.*

wife, Mathis replied, "Oh, it did for a couple of days, I guess." Meierhenry challenged Mathis, saying he had given three different stories under oath. Earlier, Mathis had said in sworn testimony that there was no relationship between him and the girl.

Meierhenry ended his cross-examination by attempting to catch Mathis off guard. Walking back toward his seat, Meierhenry stopped, turned and asked Mathis, "Did Patrick say anything before you shot him the second time?" Leaning forward in the witness chair, Mathis squinted at Meierhenry, and he replied, "What?"

Meierhenry repeated the question, and defense attorneys immediately objected. Meierhenry told Judge Anderst he had no further questions. With his voice nearly inaudible because of the intensity of the objections, Mathis responded in a low voice, "I didn't kill anybody."[106]

Mathis's testimony was followed by an expert witness from New York, who disputed the state's witnesses who said that the blood between Ladonna's and Patrick's beds was that of John Mathis. Professor Herbert MacDonell, director of laboratory and forensic sciences at Corning College in New York, said the blood was Patrick's, but admitted that he based his opinion on his background in forensic science because he did not take the blood samples themselves or test them. Meierhenry read from an interview MacDonell gave in a national publication that quoted MacDonell as saying, "I'm in the business of giving hope to the hopeless and since nobody in the world can contradict me, I have to be very, very careful." Meierhenry, commenting on MacDonell's admission that he did not look at all the photographs relevant to his findings, said to MacDonell, "It wouldn't be very, very careful now, not to look at all the pictures, would it?"[107]

The defense suffered a setback when its evidence involving the gold spray paint was shown to be faulty. The words "Mathus suck shit" were painted on the door of the shed that the Mathis family was using as a temporary home. As with the murder weapon, no paint container was found, and defense investigator Tim Mulloy, former deputy sheriff in Yankton and Union Counties, testified concerning tests he conducted in his garage to learn more about the gold paint graffiti. He said he used September 8 weather condition data provided by the National Climate Center in Asheville, North Carolina, for the Mount Vernon area. However, Meierhenry's assistant, Dennis Holmes, pointed out that the weather data submitted was for September 8, 1980, the wrong year, a fact discovered by Davison County state's attorney Pat Kiner. This revelation negated the Mulloy's tests.[108]

Meierhenry also challenged Mulloy's assertion that there were three possible suspects in the case other than Mathis, which was intended to demonstrate the defense's contention that the investigation was slipshod.

Meierhenry grilled Mulloy about why he thought the three men in question were suspects.

"You're saying Dan Pollard is a suspect?" he asked Mulloy.

"A possible suspect," Mulloy responded.

"What's a possible suspect?" wondered Meierhenry.

"Somebody who could have a motive," Mulloy said.[109]

"You're making an accusation," Meierhenry said. "What evidence do you have?"

Mulloy said he considered Pollard a potential suspect because he was engaged to Tatum and lived seven-and-a-half miles from the Mathis farm. Earlier, Pollard had testified for the state that he did not know Tatum's relationship with Mathis went beyond a single kiss until after the murders. His .22 caliber had been tested, with a negative result.

Mulloy also said the Mathises' neighbor Darris Uhre, who had been twice institutionalized in the Human Services Center, was a possible suspect and owned a .22-caliber rifle. However, Mulloy did not take the rifle. "You didn't take possession of it and you work for the defense. You know the state would have tested it for you," Meierhenry said.[110] The third possible suspect, according to Mulloy, was a drug burnout.

The defense wrapped up its case by casting doubt on the prosecution's blood tests, which concluded that blood found between Ladonna Mathis's and Patrick's beds belonged to John Mathis. Dr. MacDonell testified that the blood was Patrick's and dripped from the two-year-old's mattress. MacDonell also testified that the unspent shell found in Mathis's pocket the morning of the killings was different from the casings found at the murder scene. The letter *r* in *Super-X* was extremely muddled in the live round, whereas it was not in all but one of the spent cartridges, MacDonell said.[111]

The defense shored up MacDonell's testimony with a similar conclusion by a serologist from Buena Vista, California. Brian Wraxall from the Serological Research Institute disagreed with the FBI finding that the blood was Mathis's. Instead, Wraxall said it was Patrick's blood. Asked defense attorney Eklund, "Is there any possibility the blood between the beds came from John Mathis?" Wraxall answered, "No." But when cross-examined by deputy prosecutor Dennis Holmes, Wraxall admitted that a lapse of time would have an impact on the blood tests. However, he reiterated that he could reach a conclusion from what was submitted.[112]

The point/counterpoint over the blood found between the beds took place because the prosecution believed that Mathis shot himself in the arm between the beds after he committed the murders.[113]

The defense offered further testimony that questioned the FBI's findings on the bullets. Jeff Masten, a Canton, South Dakota attorney and Lincoln County state's attorney, said he disagreed with the FBI's conclusions on the similarities between the spent cartridges and the unspent shell found on John Mathis. He called part of the FBI analysis pertaining to arsenic in spent slugs and the live round "pure garbage."[114] Masten, who received a master's degree in theoretical physics from Columbia University, said the bullets were similar only because they were manufactured by the same company. He did, however, acknowledge that three of the four slugs were similar.

The state's assertion that Mathis intentionally damaged his watch in order to support the defendant's story about a struggle was also challenged. Ron Strom, a Sioux City, Iowa watchmaker and jeweler, said he didn't think the watch was deliberately damaged, counter to testimony by two prosecution witnesses.[115]

In an effort to negate the belief that a husband and father could murder his wife and children, the defense called on Dr. Frederick Miller of Denver, who testified that he found no reason "as to why John Mathis might have killed his wife and sons. I find it extremely unordinary and he does not demonstrate the disorders evident in other cases I have evaluated." Miller's conclusion was supported by Dr. Eugene Schwartz, a clinical psychologist from Boulder, Colorado, who told the court that as a result of his testing, he initially thought Mathis might have some sort of neurological disorder, but medical tests proved he did not. Schwartz said Mathis was a "basic, simple concrete guy whose inner life is generally impoverished."[116] Despite a rigorous cross-examination by Meierhenry, Miller stood by his contention that it was highly unusual for a parent to kill his child, saying that in his experience observing such cases, most involved a continuing history of child abuse.[117]

A damaged watch worn by John Mathis was the subject of conflicting testimony from timepiece experts. *Courtesy of the Davison County Sheriff's Department.*

As the trial reached its final stage, the prosecution called ten rebuttal witnesses, including the parents of Darris Uhre, whom defense investigator Tim Mulloy had named as a "potential suspect." Mr. and Mrs. Uhre testified that their son had a drug problem and had been institutionalized twice. Mrs. Uhre testified she knew her son was home the night and morning of the murders. A key component of the defense's case was that law enforcement had not adequately investigated suspects other than John Mathis. Mulloy had also named Dan Pollard, the fiancé of Kim Tatum, as a potential suspect, but never advanced him to the "suspect" category. Most of the other rebuttal witnesses were law enforcement officials who expanded on the state's investigation of Uhre, which had gone nowhere.[118]

Chapter 11
COURTROOM ELOQUENCE

Most lawyers in the state and indeed most legal scholars agreed that the opposing counsel in the John Mathis trial were top-tier attorneys. Mark Meierhenry and Rick Johnson were in their prime and their associates, Wally Eklund for the defense and Dennis Holmes for the state, were highly regarded as well.

Closing arguments for both sides, according to onlookers, riveted the courtroom.

The *Daily Republic* of Mitchell reported Meierhenry's comments this way:

> *Attorney General Mark Meierhenry told the jury at the John Mathis murder trial today that of all the evidence presented in the case, not a single piece indicates there was another person at the farm the night of the shootings of Ladonna Mathis and two of her children.*
>
> *"We should have saved one evidence sticker and put it on John Mathis," said Meierhenry, noting he was the most important piece of evidence in the case since the alleged assailant left him alive.*
>
> *Meierhenry asked the jury on frequent occasions in closing statements to consider why the alleged assailant would coolly kill a woman and two boys and leave Mathis alive. Holding up an artist's drawing of the alleged masked man who allegedly killed Mathis's family and wounded him, Meierhenry said, "If you take off this mask, I submit to you that you would find John Mathis. You're looking at how John Mathis was dressed that night, dark gloves, dark sweatshirt. Why would a masked man walk*

on the property, kill a woman and two children, and yet leave this man alive?" asked Meierhenry.

Pointing at Mathis, Meierhenry said, "This man, whose testimony shows he's a healthy man, fell to the ground and was unconscious 28 minutes or more. You don't have to be a fight fan to wonder about that. Twenty-eight minutes unconscious, yet you can wake up, make a call, and remember statements."

Meierhenry said the killer was efficient. "He didn't take a lot of time. He shot a little boy once in the head, very efficiently, shot a woman, very efficiently, and shot this little boy, but not quite as efficiently—he had to shoot him twice," said Meierhenry as he held up a photo of Patrick Mathis. "It's only common sense that a man who would shoot these people would confront John Mathis but not shoot him in the head and leave him for dead. That doesn't make sense. There's no motive for leaving him alive to describe the killer. Then this assailant would write childish graffiti, yet leave John Mathis with only a little wound in the arm. Why wouldn't the man walk over while John Mathis was unconscious and shoot him in the ear? Why? I submit to you there was no masked stranger," said Meierhenry.

He said the court has heard the testimony given by both prosecution and defense witnesses saying the Mathises were not a particularly social family, leaving no one to dislike them. He also asked the jury to question in their minds how many people would have been able to find the Mathis family in the shed that night.

"Who in the whole wide world would know? Who would be able to stop their car, make their way onto the farm yard, into the shop, find the light and kill three people," asked Meierhenry.

"We have no videotape of the crime, so we have to go by the facts. We have to look at all the facts and find them consistent with one thing. John Mathis killed his wife and children."

Meierhenry touched on the subject of Kim Tatum, a neighbor woman who testified that Mathis had kissed her three or four times and felt the private parts of her body. "Maybe in the rigid, concrete mind of his, he said, 'If I can get rid of my wife and children, I can do what I want,'" said Meierhenry. "I think the evidence shows he cared more for his hogs than he did his family."

Meierhenry reviewed for the jury what he considered other evidence against Mathis: the bullet found in Mathis's pocket, which was the same caliber as the casings found at the murder scene. "What are the odds that

Sheriffs Department

DAVISON COUNTY
P.O. Box 819
MITCHELL, SOUTH DAKOTA 57301

YLE W. SWENSON, Sheriff
Phone 605, 996-7797

September 14, 1981

SECRET WITNESS LINE

This is a rumor that was passed onto me late this afternoon, this is Friday afternoon and if it has not been pursued by the Sheriff's Department, perhaps it would be worth looking into. Someone told me that they had heard that some of these people who have been arrested on drug charges had been at the Mathis home sometime recently and that the Mathis' had reported them, and consequently we suggesting that this maybe something to help solve the mystery of the murdered. I don't know anything definite but felt it was worth calling in and giving this information. Thank you.

A Secret Witness telephone line was established to aid law enforcement in gathering information on the murders. Each call was transcribed and filed. *Courtesy of the Davison County Sheriff's Department.*

the day before a 2-year-old boy and a 4-year-old boy were shot in the head that your 4-year-old found a shell in the yard. How do you explain it?" Meierhenry asked.[119]

Then Meierhenry reminded the jury of other key prosecution points. The gunshot in Mathis's arm was consistent with a self-inflicted wound. John Mathis may be "dull normal," but not talking about the shell found in his pocket for forty-two days? "That's consistent with guilt."

"Forty-two days went by and Mr. Mathis never mentioned to anyone about the bullet until I asked at the grand jury," Meierhenry said.

Mathis was heard to say his wife was a hard worker, Meierhenry said, but never did he say that he loved her. And, Meierhenry emphasized, no blood was found around the area Mathis said he was shot. "Sometimes what's not there is as important as what is there," he said.[120]

Meierhenry took pains to explain to the jury the importance of circumstantial evidence, offering the example of a new concrete driveway with large dog tracks marring the surface. No one saw the neighbor's dog walk in the concrete, Meierhenry said. No one heard him bark. But the dog had cement on his feet. There wasn't any doubt that the neighbor's St. Bernard dog had walked in the cement. "It could have been a dog 10 miles away…but is it reasonable?"[121]

Then it was the defense's turn, with Johnson telling the jury, "When I sit down, there will be nothing more that can help John Mathis in this case. You will hold exclusively the power to destroy him."[122]

Johnson and Eklund shared the closing argument duties. This from the *Daily Republic*:

> Eklund hit often on the role the jury was about to play in the future of Mathis, but also spent a good amount of time alleging a sloppy investigation by the state and on several occasions took the liberty of bringing inferences about prosecuting attorney Mark Meierhenry's involvement in a gambling incident into the argument. In his closing arguments, Meierhenry used the theme, "no one in the whole wide world" to set the stage for his summation to the jury while Johnson drove home the betting angle, hinting at the prosecuting attorney's liking the idea of playing a betting game.
>
> In concluding, Johnson walked to where Mathis was sitting and turned to the jury: "He will be sitting here. You will have to look at this man and look him in the eye and say you are a cold blooded murderer and the evidence is all here."
>
> Johnson said it was unfair in asking the jury to "make a mistake in destroying a man's life." He briefly mentioned the bullet in Mathis's pocket, his watch and the blood around and on Mathis when he awoke from the alleged assault, something the defense has tied their whole case together with. He only briefly brought up the testimony of Kim Tatum, the young woman who Mathis kissed "three or four times."
>
> With a raised voice, Johnson got the attention of the 15 jurors, asking them to consider the investigation into the deaths of Ladonna, Patrick and Brian Mathis as one blundered by the law enforcement officers—an aspect he spent most of his time on. Referring to Meierhenry, he noted, "He used

three or four references to odds. I know as attorney general he is interested in odds. But if you folks are, I am sadly disappointed. This is no horse race, this is no blackjack game. If the odds are what he wants you to decide on, then you have to vote John Mathis innocent if one odd is in his favor."

Noting Meierhenry's reference to the fact that Mathis did not mention he loved Ladonna on the stand and that his hogs were more important to him than his family, Johnson asked the jurors, "Look back at the evidence, the witnesses, their circumstances. Now that's a peculiar statement to make, indicating those people told of the Mathises as not being unfriendly to each other and caring for the children."

"They came in here and to ask you to destroy him because of this kind of trash. And they ought to be embarrassed. It shows you how far they have stooped in this case—that he liked his hogs better than his children. They brought up barroom talk. Did his wife go to church that Sunday. So find him guilty for that. So he didn't have a nice toilet for his family. So Mr. Meierhenry says 'find him guilty.'"

Johnson took issue with the tests conducted by officers investigating the crime and alleged Meierhenry put words in Mathis's mouth with the idea that the alleged assailant was lefthanded and the time knocked out on the ground was 28 minutes. "He says it couldn't have been that long. Well, I don't qualify Mr. Meierhenry as a doctor."

He criticized the use of a psychic and wondered why the prosecution faulted the defendant for remembering the names of nurses. "So that's a reason to get rid of him?" Johnson asked.

"Then they bring up all the baloney about the fires. They want to show you there is something suspicious about it. I urge you to take a close look at instruction number 13 on your sheet and consider reasonable doubt and moral certainty. You cannot write 'guilty' on the ballots unless you are morally certain."

Johnson also picked up on Meierhenry's example of dog tracks in wet concrete to illustrate circumstantial evidence. "His law officers never even bothered to look at the dog tracks. His officers never even checked the size of the dog tracks," he said.[123]

Meierhenry, when closing out the proceeding with his rebuttal statement, condemned Johnson's reference to Meierhenry's personal life and the gambling episode in a Winner bar in 1979. Though he criticized Johnson's reference to the incident, Meierhenry then told the jury: "He (Mathis) has the best possible defense. He has two fine lawyers arguing his case."

Meierhenry said the defense had attempted "to strike your sympathy rather than steer you to the facts of the case."

"In all of their 2½ hour argument, they dismissed the shell in Mathis's pocket, the wristwatch, the lack of blood where Mathis says he was attacked in less than three minutes."

Countering the defense's assertion that the jurors had the power to destroy Mathis, Meierhenry said: "You have not destroyed him. He has destroyed himself."[124]

Assistant attorney general Holmes recapped the scientific evidence about bullets, Mathis's wound in the arm and the lack of blood on Mathis's shirt where he said he rested his arm after being shot by the assailant. Referring to the blood between Ladonna's and Patrick's beds, Holmes told the jury: "He either shot himself there or had to throw Patrick back up onto the bed after he shot him. That's for you to decide."[125]

Eklund, in his part of the defense's summation, told the jury that Mathis's statements "were consistent as the state wishes their evidence was. That's inconsistent with guilt." He accused the state of leaving behind evidence. "If it didn't fit their intentions of finding John guilty, they left it. As jurors, you are entitled to be the witnesses as to whether they are testifying truthfully or not."[126]

Chapter 12

JURY DELIBERATES

When the four attorneys for the prosecution and defense completed their closing statements on Monday, May 10, jurors spent two hours in the early evening considering what they had heard that day and the evidence presented in the monthlong murder trial that began on April 12. Judge Thomas Anderst excused three alternate jurors who had sat through the trial and thanked them for their service.

"The solution is now in the hands of 12 Yankton County people who deliberated for 2½ hours Monday before retiring at about 8:40 p.m. The jurors will be sequestered in a local motel until they return a verdict in the case," the Sioux Falls *Argus Leader* reported.[127]

Mathis, who had been free throughout on a $300,000 property bond, seemed undisturbed by the final stage of the trial. Asked if the crowd was getting on his nerves, he said, "No, it's when nobody's around that it gets bad." Mathis took it in stride when he heard that a bailiff was arranging hotel accommodations for the jury Tuesday night. He said he'd been told about the legal adage that says the longer a jury is out, the better chance a defendant has.[128]

Judge Anderst offered his thoughts on the jury as he spoke to a pre-law seminar at Mount Marty College. "I expect the deliberations will be lengthy," the judge said. "I think they're all strong individuals with strong minds. I think they're going to speak out, and hold their positions." While he waited for the jury, Anderst also wrote his instructions on the death penalty in case the jury found Mathis guilty. Meierhenry had said early on that he would ask for the death penalty.[129]

By the third day of deliberations, one of the bailiffs said that he noted increased tension in the jurors as the hours passed. John Mathis was characteristically silent, but his father, Vern, said his son "is crying on the inside through every minute of this."

The jurors, who had been housed at the Flamming Court motel near the Public Safety Center, checked into the Skyline Motel on Tuesday, apparently because the first motel didn't have room for all of them.

Then, after approximately two-and-a-half days of deliberation, jurors decided on Wednesday afternoon, May 12, 1982, that John Mathis was not guilty of murdering his wife and two sons.

They had reached the decision at a quarter after four in the afternoon.

At the judge's request, foreman Gary Honomichl read the verdict. Defense counsel Johnson placed his arms around Mathis and whispered a quiet phrase to his client, who stood silently. Holmes, twenty-seven-year-old assistant attorney general, sat rocking in his chair, quietly looking forward. Davison county state's attorney Pat Kiner sat at the prosecution table, pen in hand, writing nothing.[130]

Later in the day, Honomichl was home relaxing with his family. He said that the experience, while good, was "a hardship for a man, on mind and body." He said jurors laid out all the trial evidence Monday evening after they were locked in Courtroom A. The first ballot was eight not guilty, three guilty and one undecided. After two more ballots were taken, the jury's vote had changed to nine not guilty, two guilty and one undecided. A later vote came in at 10–2, and on Wednesday, the vote was 11–1. Finally, just after four o'clock on Wednesday, the verdict was unanimous for acquittal.[131]

A slightly different account was reported by the *Argus Leader*. It quoted Honomichl as saying the jury took five ballots. The first was seven not guilty, three guilty and two undecided. The second was nine not guilty, three guilty. The third, ten not guilty and two guilty. The fourth, eleven not guilty and one guilty. And the fifth, twelve not guilty.

When the verdict was read, John Mathis walked to the jury box, reached out and shook the hand of juror Patricia Holmes, then Deanna Erickson, then Jane King. He stopped at the entrance of the jury room and spoke a few words to juror Barbara Bosch, then went into the room where the jury had been empaneled nearly twenty-four hours over the past three days. Later, Mathis stood in the hallway outside the jury room and talked to the news media who had covered the case. "Relieved" was his only answer when asked how he felt. What went through his mind when the jury foreman stood? "I was just hoping. I was praying for it."[132]

Mathis said he never considered the possibility of what he would have done if it had gone the other way. "I guess I never thought about it because I never thought it could happen. I knew this was the way it was supposed to go." He also said he had done all he could to help law enforcement find the murderer. "I don't know what else I can do, but if I can, I'll try."[133]

Johnson said later, "It was a classic murder trial. There was never one single piece of hard evidence that proved it either way—guilt or innocence. Neither side could ever feel comfortable with the evidence." But he said, "All I can say is that lawyers don't win or lose cases, clients do." Law partner Eklund described his emotion as "sheer elation." Then he added, "We deserved to win."[134]

Outside the courtroom, in the crowded second-floor lobby of the Yankton Safety Center, Johnson spoke into the microphones of tape recorders and television cameras, expounding on the innocence of his most famous client. But one Yankton woman, who had sat through the trial, stood across the hall and marveled at the scene, hand over her mouth, speaking quietly. "I think it's just terrible. Now, I can say it." It was an indication that not everyone who had followed the trial agreed with the jury's verdict.[135]

An obviously disappointed Meierhenry stared out the window of the public safety building. "I'm not going to make any statements of disgust, anger or regret," he said. "We went through the system and the system worked…the jury decided the evidence wasn't there."[136]

"We have to presume there is this mysterious masked man out in the Mount Vernon area somewhere now," Meierhenry said. The case had to be tried, and the state's job was "to prove without a reasonable doubt and the jury decided the evidence wasn't there. So I guess the case remains open. I don't know of any leads to be followed."[137]

Meierhenry wouldn't second-guess himself or how the case was handled. He said he wouldn't try the case any differently if he had the opportunity to do it again. Meanwhile, Sheriff Swenson was more pointed about the verdict, saying that justice had not been served. He had to say this, he said, because his investigation led him to believe that Mathis was guilty. "The case is open," Swenson said, but not much would happen unless new evidence turned up. "We're going to leave the file open but we have absolutely no other leads. We gave the people 1,000 percent of what we had. We brought in every investigator possible. I stand by the investigation," said a disappointed Swenson.

Defense attorney Johnson, perhaps anticipating some negative public reaction following the verdict, said he was tired of the prejudiced public.

Meierhenry: Truth may never be brought out

MARK MEIERHENRY

YANKTON, S.D. (AP) — No new evidence has turned up the past year in the killings of LaDonna Mathis and two of her sons at their Mount Vernon farm, says Attorney General Mark Meierhenry.

It was a year ago that a Yankton County jury found John Mathis innocent of three counts of murder in the shooting deaths of his wife and two pre-school age sons.

"We're not actively looking for anyone. We will accept any evidence that comes in, but there have been no new leads since that time," Meierhenry said. "We have not been informed that any of the rewards, I think it's up to $25,000 that Mathis had out, has revealed any information. I think the jury here in Yankton County got all the information that law enforcement's ever going to have as to who committed that crime."

Meierhenry was the chief prosecutor in the case against Mathis, who said a masked man attacked him and his family that Sept. 8, 1981 night.

Meierhenry said the justice system is not perfect.

"I would like to say that every crime is solved, every guilty man is brought to justice, and that our system never makes a mistake. But we know all three of those things aren't true," he said.

Meierhenry said the case against Mathis was handled properly by the prosecution and he has accepted the jury's verdict.

"Right after the trial I said I can live with it and I can live with it today, and I'm not going to look over my shoulder. There's more in the future."

News story. *Lyle Swenson collection.*

"I keep hearing friends of mine or whatever saying, 'I really think he did it but I don't think the state can prove it.' That's a contradiction in terms and it rags me a little. John shouldn't come out of this deal any way but innocent. I hope they'll put it to bed," he said.[138]

Mount Vernon residents reacted with stunned silence to the jury's judgment, according to the *Daily Republic*, which sent a reporter to gauge the community sentiment.

Most residents would not comment, at least not on the record, but a few did. Pete Greibel, who lived north of Mount Vernon not far from the Mathis farm, said, "There's a lot of wondering what's going on. But there was no evidence to prove he did it. You can't nail a guy from something you can't prove." Then he added, "Something will show up later. I don't think they're going to give up on this." Joan Hegg, a resident of the town, said she "didn't expect it; it's rather shocking. But if they don't have the evidence, that's the way it's going to come out."[139]

The triple murders, grand jury findings and the run-up to the trial captured the public's attention, and as the *Associated Press* reported the day after the not guilty verdict, authorities were hard-pressed to explain some aspects of the state's most horrific crime.

The verdict came exactly one month after the trial opened in Yankton, and the state zeroed in on Mathis's quasi-sexual relationship with a neighbor girl and an unspent .22-caliber bullet found in his pocket. It also contended that Mathis cared more about his farm work and hogs than his family. The defense argued the state's evidence was circumstantial. No murder weapon was found, and their experts testified that Mathis wasn't smart enough to plan and execute such a crime. When Mathis himself told the courtroom he wished he had died so he could be with his family, it evidently helped sway the jury to his side.

What the public did not know when the verdict was rendered was that jurors had been influenced by the discovery of a spent .22-caliber casing on a Yankton sidewalk as they were walking during a supper break on Monday, the first day of deliberations.

"It was lying on the sidewalk, plain as day," jury foreman Honomichl said, his eyes still widening, his voice still incredulous. "I just said, 'Look at that!' One of the girls said, 'Good gravy.'" The shell was a Winchester Western .22-caliber Super X, the same brand of shells used to kill Ladonna Mathis and her two sons.[140]

Rifle bullets played a central role in the prosecution's case against Mathis. It was established that .22-caliber bullets had been used to kill the three victims. While the defense attempted to discredit testimony that tied the unspent bullet in John Mathis's pocket to the ones used in the killings, there was no question what kind of gun or ammunition was used.

Juror Burnell Haugen said he was dumbfounded at seeing the shell. "They were using all these odds and all the probables and then here he found one on the sidewalk right in town. It really exploited that part." Though jurors interviewed said the shell had a significant impact on them, all seven of those interviewed said they acquitted the thirty-year-old hog farmer because there was no proof he was guilty.[141] After the shell, the most significant obstacle to acquittal was the smashed wristwatch found on Mathis's arm.

In April 2021, Jon Erickson, an assistant attorney general in charge of coordinating the evidence for the state who went on to become a circuit court judge, said he believed the rifle cartridges were planted.

"When the jury went out to deliberate, it was to a restaurant that was in an old library. And there was a circular sidewalk and they found a .22 bullet on each side. The bailiff collected them and they were tested. They were not fired. The bullets had been pulled out of the casings.

"Speculation was that someone left them there because part of the trial was that you could find .22 shells anywhere. They placed them on either side of the sidewalk so the jurors would see one of them. I personally don't feel that Rick or Wally had anything to do with it, but I do think it was a plant. And that was because someone had pulled the bullets out of the casings. They were not fired bullets."

Erickson believes if the prosecution had found the gun, "it would have made a big difference.

"It is one of those cases that just haunts you. What more could we have done? It's all that 20/20 hindsight."

Haugen, forty-four, was the last holdout for a guilty verdict. Honomichl, thirty-nine, was next. Both men said they weren't necessarily saying Mathis was innocent—just not guilty under the law.

All seven jurors said they discounted the testimony of Kim Tatum, who said she had a quasi-sexual relationship with Mathis. "She was only 14 and she said she was his babysitter," juror Elmer Hauck said. "Why would a man want to mingle with a young girl like that for? Something would have to be wrong with him, and besides, he testified he didn't."[142]

Juror Ray Harris, thirty-one, said he dismissed the Tatum testimony because he believes all people have skeletons in their closets. He also said he didn't think Mathis was cunning enough to conceive and carry out the crime. Juror Terri Beavers, thirty-six, said she felt it was possible that it happened like Mathis said. "Not necessarily probable but possible. There were no facts to find him innocent and no facts to find him guilty. So under the law you have to presume him innocent."

Two other jurors, Deanna Erickson and Jane King, had no doubts about Mathis's innocence. "I believe he was telling the truth. I don't think everyone on the jury is convinced he was innocent, but I was," King said.[143]

Chapter 13

NOT GUILTY, BUT NOT FREE

In an interview a year after his acquittal, John Mathis said he didn't feel like a free man.

"If you could put yourself in my spot, you'd know how it feels," he said. "So I guess the answer is no, I don't feel like a free man."[144]

The house that was under construction at the time his wife and two sons were murdered was completed. Mathis said he had tried to do some of the things Ladonna had wanted, like have a lamp in the window. He had kept her clothing and personal belongings, and he was continuing his hog-farming operation. He was still offering the $25,000 reward—increased from the original $10,000—for information about the assailant he said killed his family and wounded him on September 8, 1981. "I still have hopes that the murderer will be apprehended. When it does happen, I don't know about it coming together piece by piece. I think it'll happen all at once," he said. Asked if he thought there were people who still thought the jury in Yankton was wrong, he responded, "People can think what they want to and if they can't live with it, it's their problem."[145]

Attorney General Meierhenry said no new evidence had been unearthed in the years since the trial and that the investigation was inactive. "We will accept any new evidence that comes in, but there have been no new leads." He added, "I would like to say that every crime is solved, every guilty man is brought to justice and that our system never makes a mistake. But we know all three of those things aren't true. Right after the trial I said I can live with it and I can live with it today. I'm not going to look over my shoulder. There's more in the future."[146]

Law enforcement and the state prosecution team gathered during the Mathis murder trial. Front row, from left: Dennis Holmes, Mark Meierhenry and Lyle Swenson. Back row, from left: Jon Erickson, Ken Giegling, Doug Kirkus and David Muller. *Courtesy of the Davison County Sheriff's Department.*

In the decades following the trial, media outlets marked the case with regular updates. In September 1984, the Sioux Falls *Argus Leader* headline said, "Mathis case still haunts the books." The story quotes Kirkus, the Davison County deputy sheriff Mathis telephoned first.

"There is hardly a day goes by that I don't think about it or something brings it to my attention," Kirkus said. "When I drive by the farm and see the machine shed, I can see people lying there today."

Davison County sheriff Swenson is quoted in the story as saying the case "was solved as far as we were concerned, I mean law enforcement.…We believed we had the right man, and we prosecuted on that basis. The biggest mystery remains the missing murder weapon. Several .22 rifles have been tested since the verdict, but nothing panned out."

Johnson, the Gregory defense lawyer, said people mentioned the case to him almost daily. Tim Mulloy, who was hired by the defense as an investigator, said he continues to track down leads from those who contact him or Mathis. "[Mathis] is sincere in his desire to find the killer," Mulloy said.

For Evelyn and Lorenz Gerlach, Ladonna's parents, the outcome of the trial still baffles them. "We feel the court was unjust and we were terribly, terribly hurt," Evelyn said. "John is guilty and that is all we know."

In 1991, the *Argus* published another September update; this time, the headline declared, "A case unsolved." The story described John Mathis as one unkindly marked by the passage of time since the triple slaying ten years earlier: "His shiny brown hair has dulled. His face has weathered, his jowls filled. He looks tired and sad." Mathis beat the charges, the story continued, but public opinion had been a more resilient enemy. His conviction had sentenced Mathis to a life of exile on his Davison County farm, a man tolerated but never accepted or acknowledged.

An accompanying story related how Lorenz and Evelyn Gerlach were dealing with the murder of their daughter and two of their grandsons. "Nobody paid a penalty or apologized for anything," said Lorenz. He and Evelyn remained convinced that the murderer was their son-in-law, John Mathis.

Mulloy, investigator for the defense, said Mathis's son Duane, who was staying with the Gerlachs at the time of the murders, "is adjusting pretty well." In fact, Duane was the greatest testimony to his father's innocence, Mulloy said. "Why would John Mathis kill his family and raise a kid?"

The *Argus* story also quoted Judge Anderst as saying the case might never die. Both Anderst and jury foreman Honomichl, according to the story, said they had no question the proper verdict was rendered.

"There's not one doubt," said Honomichl. However, in a sidebar story on the principals in the case, Honomichl said he had a good idea who the real murderer was. The problem, according to the story, was that Honomichl was not telling. The story also said that several years earlier, Honomichl said he talked with a man who convinced him that the Mathis slayings were part of a larger mystery. But he never went to authorities with his information and doubted he ever would. The story did not explain why.

Honomichl died in September 2020 at age seventy-seven.

The *Daily Republic* of Mitchell updated the story on September 7, 1996, with the headline "15 years later, Mathis deaths still unsolved." The case, perhaps the most notorious in the state's history, remains open, the story said, and quoted Sheriff Swenson as saying, "The longer it goes, the less possibility there is of bringing a resolve to the case." John Mathis declined to talk to the newspaper. He was still living on the family farm.

Horror in the Heartland

Five years later, on September 8, 2001, the Mitchell newspaper displayed a front-page story, "The Mathis murders: 20 years ago today," featuring Lorenz and Evelyn Gerlach. A photo of the couple holding pictures of their daughter and two slain grandsons ran with the story, as did a photo of Davison County sheriff Kim Moline. Moline was holding a drawing of a masked man as described by John Mathis. Evelyn Gerlach said the crime and its memory "would always hurt, but it scars much worse this way." She said she could hardly believe that the case had not been resolved. "I always thought that the law would do something for us, but nobody did," she said.

Former sheriff Swenson said in hindsight there was not a lot he could have done differently in building the case. Kirkus, a deputy at the time, said perhaps some things could have been handled differently, but he doubted that it would have changed the outcome of the trial. Kirkus said one weak point in the state's case was the lack of a clear-cut motive for the murders. Honomichl said, "We did what we had to do with the evidence that we had. It was a real hard decision. A few people were undecided."

Since the trial, the Gerlachs have not had contact with John Mathis or his son, Duane, who was an infant and staying with the Gerlachs at the time of the murders. Sadly, the Gerlachs said, they doubt that the case will ever be resolved—and their only wish can never be granted. "We'd like to have her back," Evelyn Gerlach said.

Thirty years after the murders, on September 8, 2011, the *Daily Republic* printed another update, headlined: "We arrested the right man." The story again quoted Swenson and Kirkus as saying they thought the right person was arrested. The story brought out some points that earlier stories had omitted. One was the spent Super X shell that jurors found on the sidewalk as they returned from supper on the first evening of deliberation, which bolstered the defense's argument that such bullets were common and scattered everywhere. The prosecution claimed the bullet was planted. Swenson said he believed that was what happened.

The story also described Swenson's contact with New Jersey psychic Dorothy Allison. Swenson said Allison knew he was calling from a place with a horrific smell when he called her from the Mathis's hog unit. She also smelled smoke, although she didn't know of the two fires at the Mathis home. And Allison saw a series of numbers that made no sense to her but were tied to the case. Swenson said after he hung up the phone, he was startled to see that the numbers she recited matched the license plate on Mathis's pickup. Despite Allison's interest in the case, and Swenson's interest in Allison's claims, the prosecution wanted no part of it.

Meierhenry said the prosecution could not overcome a deep-seated belief among people that a man would not harm or kill his own children. "As I look back I would have recognized that at that time there was a myth, a myth that parents could not harm their children, No. 1," Meierhenry said. "No. 2, that sometimes myth overwhelms reason because that's what we all want to believe."

The story prompted an unanticipated reaction. Duane Mathis, who was an infant at the time of the murders, was raised by his father. Now thirty, Duane contacted the newspaper and proclaimed his father's innocence.

"I don't believe he did it," Duane said, in his first-ever interview about the murders. "If he did it, I wouldn't still be here."

Duane described growing up with his father as tough, at times, because his father was a hard worker and expected the same of his son. But he said he never suffered anything worse than spankings, "no beat-downs or anything like that." When the story was published on September 10, 2011, Duane was living in the home that was being built at the time of the slayings. The machine shed still stood, but Duane said its presence didn't bother him. "I wasn't there, so I don't think of it every time I walk out there." He said he and his father have discussed the murders, but only rarely and briefly, and he believes his father has suffered silently.

Duane referred to the regular media stories on the anniversary of the murders and said he has been angry at what he considers one-sided coverage. He said that the masked man his father said was the assailant "never gets brought up," and he wants people to know there is another side to the story. "You've got to know the person before you actually accuse them," he said. "Don't judge a book by its cover."

Chapter 14

UNRESOLVED

Forty years after Ladonna Mathis and two of her sons were shot to death, the case remains unsolved.

No one was ever punished for their deaths.

The lone suspect, Ladonna's husband, John Mathis, was acquitted by a Yankton County jury after a monthlong trial. Though his family offered a reward for information leading to the arrest of the perpetrator, the reward went unclaimed.

Those involved with the prosecution of the case continued to believe, in the years following, that John Mathis was guilty, in spite of the jury's verdict. Those involved in Mathis's defense believed the jury made the right decision. The jurors themselves, at least the ones who commented, believed in what they did.

John Mathis is retired and living in Mitchell. When contacted in October 2020 and asked if he would discuss the case in order to ensure a balanced report and to include his perspective after four decades, Mathis said, "That's not going to happen."

Then he added, "If law enforcement had done their job, there wouldn't even have been a trial. Take it from there."

Meierhenry, attorney general of South Dakota at the time he prosecuted the case, said more than once that he believed the right person had been charged. When a new cold case unit was established as part of the state's Department of Criminal Investigation in 2004, Meierhenry said, "It would be a waste of resources to look for somebody else in that case."[147]

$10,000.00 REWARD

Offered for information leading to the arrest and conviction of the person or persons responsible for the murders of Ladonna Mathis, Brian Mathis and Patrick Mathis.

Contact: Gerrit Brink 236-5670 or 942-4541
Reward not available to Law Enforcement Officers.

A newspaper advertisement offering a reward—never claimed—for information leading to the arrest of the "masked man" who murdered Ladonna Mathis and two of her sons. Courtesy of the Davison County Sheriff's Department.

"The finding wasn't that the person on trial was the wrong person; he was not guilty because the jury didn't believe the state had proved its case."

Sixteen years later, in an interview in March 2020, only four months before he died, Meierhenry said jury verdicts reflect life. "I thought I had my finger on the pulse of the jurors," he said. "Before I went down [to Yankton], we decided we wanted father figures, and Mathis is guilty. And there isn't a jury that won't convict. The evidence is there. Was overwhelming, someone who flips his cork and kills his family.

"Now we go to this good Catholic community of Yankton, a nice little community. Well, when they got on that jury—and I found out afterward—the very people I depended on was faith over facts. They followed their belief that a father would never do that to children.

"As opposed to facts on the table, faith over fact. When it comes to voting [jurors balloting], a father will not do that."

Meierhenry said he thought authorities "did everything right. Of that whole affair, we all did what we should have done. We didn't have any ruined evidence and Rick defended properly. There's still a controversy about the jury finding that shell. Law enforcement is a little more cynical than I am. But it wouldn't have made any difference if I'm right on my belief theory."

All was joy in July 1981 when Mount Vernon residents celebrated the town's centennial. The mood would change two months later. *Courtesy of Doug Kirkus.*

An aerial view of Mount Vernon. *Courtesy of Doug Kirkus.*

The strain placed on the long friendship between Meierhenry and Johnson finally was repaired, but as Meierhenry recalls, "It took my wife and Rick's wife to get us to talk to each other."

Others on the prosecution side generally agreed with Meierhenry's assessment.

Now retired, former Davison County sheriff Swenson, eighty-six, started his law enforcement career in 1951 as a deputy sheriff. He was elected sheriff in 1954 and served until 1997, when he was appointed U.S. marshal. During that long career, he was supported and praised by those from both political parties and often ran unopposed for reelection.

Asked in March 2020 if there was any reason to believe that someone other than John Mathis had killed Ladonna Mathis and her two sons, he replied without hesitation, "No, not a thing. My mind hasn't changed since the day we decided John Mathis was responsible. The jury didn't buy it. So then, it's still there."

The investigation was as complete as law enforcement could manage, Swenson said. "We didn't leave a log unturned. Remember we talked to a psychic early on? I asked Dorothy Allison if it would make any difference if I called from the farm, where the murder scene was—but making sure I didn't tell her anything that you wanted her to tell you. The first thing she said was, 'I smell smoke.' Remember, the farmhouse had burned down. She said if you'll pay expenses, I'll fly out and move in with Vern Sr., and he'll tell me before we're done. But Meierhenry didn't want anything to do with psychic stuff, because he knew what would happen at trial. And he was right, but I was willing to take that chance." Then Swenson added, "The media would have made a circus out of it."

Swenson recalls that the defense raised the point that investigators did not check Mathis's pickup engine at the scene to see if it was warm, which would have indicated if it had been recently driven. Had that been done, and if the engine was warm, it could have supported the theory that someone had driven away and disposed of the murder weapon.

"We didn't check the engine when we first arrived on the scene to see if it was warm. We didn't have any reason to disbelieve John at the moment," Swenson said.

In April 2020, Kirkus, then sixty-eight, who was deputy sheriff at the time of the slayings and first on the scene, said that "I'll go to my grave believing he was guilty."

One thing Kirkus has thought about over the years is whether the jury would have come to a different decision if Mathis had been charged with killing his wife and not the children.

"Why didn't they just charge John with one murder and then down the road charge him with the others?" Kirkus wondered. It's one of many questions that he and others involved in the case have pondered over time.

That question was answered by Holmes, deputy attorney general at the time and Meierhenry's deputy prosecutor for the trial.

"I don't recall ever discussing it," Holmes said in 2020. "Legally, I don't think it was something we could have done. It was not a viable option. In my opinion, he could not have been later charged with separate homicide counts."

But what if the gun had been found later?

"Finding new evidence does not alter the double jeopardy protections of the Constitution," Holmes said. "Once a person's liberty has been placed in 'jeopardy' by a trial, they cannot be charged with that offense again, no matter what new evidence surfaces."

The questions that handicapped the state's case early on remain unanswered today: What happened to the murder weapon? What was the motive for killing a farm wife and two of her children?

The state believed that John Mathis had disposed of the gun after committing the murders and before calling Kirkus to come to the farm. Or, some theorized, he had help. Someone disposed of the gun for John Mathis, perhaps in Lake Mitchell, not far from the Mathis property, where it would never be found.

The defense attorneys argued a different scenario: there was a masked man, as Mathis said at the scene when Kirkus arrived and later in testimony at trial. The masked assailant shot Mathis's family and shot him in the arm when Mathis tried to stop him. When he left, he took the gun with him. Mathis testified he heard an engine running nearby before he confronted the assailant.

While both explanations seemed plausible to jurors, one was untrue. However, the plausibility of the masked man had planted the seed of reasonable doubt in the minds of the jurors. At first, a few jurors voted to find John Mathis guilty. But after five ballots, a not guilty verdict was unanimous.

But what about motive? If there was a masked intruder, what possible motive would he have to kill Ladonna Mathis and two of her boys? And why would he simply wound John Mathis and not kill him as well?

SOUTH DAKOTA'S MATHIS MURDERS

Office of Sheriff
Davison County

SHERIFF
LYLE W. SWENSON

210 East 4th ★ P. O. Box 819 ★ Mitchell, SD 57301
605-996-7797 ★ FAX 605-996-4651

CHIEF DEPUTY
R. KIM MOLINE

May 2, 1995

DuWayne Nitschke, Deputy
Cass County Sheriff's Office
Investigative Division
P.O. Box 488
Fargo, ND 58107

RE: Your file #I-94-00528

Dear Deputy Nitschke:

I am returning by UPS the Marlin 22 rifle, model 60, serial #15360800 that was submitted to our Office for test firing last June as per our request. I have enclosed a copy of the test results for your information.

I would like to apologize for the long delay in getting this back to you and also thank you for your great cooperation in our effort to find the right gun. As you can see it is not the gun we are looking for but we just keep trying and sooner or later we might get lucky.

Again our thanks and if we can ever be of like assistance to you or your Office please feel free to call us.

Sincerely,

Lyle W. Swenson
Sheriff

Numerous .22-caliber rifles were tested in an effort to locate the murder weapon. Another negative test result was acknowledged in this May 2, 1995 letter by Davison County sheriff Lyle Swenson nearly fourteen years after the murders. *Courtesy of the Davison County Sheriff's Department.*

The state used this very question to attack John Mathis's "masked man" version of events. Since there was no motive, the state argued, there could have been no mysterious assailant.

Jurors contacted soon after the trial, and even years later, said they stood by their decision. One, the jury foreman Gary Honomichl, went even further.

He was quoted in the September 2, 1991 Sioux Falls *Argus Leader* as saying he knew what had happened.

Honomichl said the murders involved much more than authorities knew, including a drug ring. But he wouldn't elaborate or share his theory with authorities.

"It goes so far beyond the murders," he said.

Furthermore, "a weapon on the premises and fingerprints might have reversed" the jury verdict, Honomichl said.

Honomichl, who died in September 2020, apparently never publicly discussed his theory. When his wife, Dianne, was asked in December 2020 if he had ever discussed his theory with her, she said no.

"Not really, he just said he didn't feel that John was smart enough to do it."

Though it cannot be known for sure, Honomichl may have been referring to a theory outlined by the defense's investigator, Tim Mulloy, who said in a 2021 interview that a party near the Mathis farm could have been connected to the killings.

Mulloy said a group of college and high school students were partying at an abandoned building and were discovered by a sheriff's deputy, who called the highway patrol for help. Law enforcement surrounded the building.

"The story was out that other guys in town that were in drugs lost a lot of money because a great number of these kids were busted over this and they were mad about it. Because it happened by the John Mathis house, word was that Mathis was working with the cops and it came out that somebody was going to put a bounty out on Mathis.

"We didn't say it was the actual story," said Mulloy, "but it was one of our defenses that it could possibly be."

None of this story came from John Mathis, Mulloy said.

"In theory, the masked intruder was someone involved in drug trade or a reward out to take care of Mathis."

Though Mulloy's speculation wasn't used as part of the defense, there was a growing awareness of the drug problem in South Dakota. A month before jury selection in Yankton, Meierhenry appeared before the legislature's Joint Appropriations Committee and asked for additional funds to hire

Veteran investigator Tim Mulloy was hired by the Mathis defense team. *Dave Fuller drawing.*

three more drug enforcement agents. "If we're going to have tough laws, let's go out and enforce them," Meierhenry said.[148]

Asked if he thought John Mathis was innocent, Mulloy said, "I can't say either way if he was innocent. They didn't prove him guilty."

Mulloy said the prosecution had several obstacles.

"Everything they said he did or didn't do you just had to recognize what they were and prove them wrong. In general terms, throughout the entire trial, there were factors in the case that we had to prove up that he didn't do it or that there was another reason other than him. In our mind, if they found one thing he was lying about, he would be found guilty, just because of the enormity of the case."

Mulloy believed that the state thought it had "a dead-bang winner, and that all we were doing was blowing smoke, but they eventually got a little grumpy with us because things weren't going their way.

"The story he gave about an intruder attacking him, shooting him in the arm, they thought that was impossible."

Mulloy, as a witness for the defense, had mentioned a "drug burnout" as a possible suspect, which angered Meierhenry.

"You threw out the drug thing. Are you making accusations that John Mathis was involved in drug traffic? You haven't heard the state allege Mr. Mathis was involved in drugs, have you?" Meierhenry asked Mulloy.[149]

"No sir," Mulloy responded.

But the implication of illegal drugs playing a role in the case had circulated from the outset.

Another story involved the landing of an airplane on a makeshift runway in Walworth County on January 20, 1980. It was loaded with twenty-six thousand pounds of baled Colombian marijuana. The plan was to land in a remote area and take the marijuana to the Twin Cities for distribution. However, five ice fishermen saw the plane land, thought it was suspicious and drove to the site.[150]

One of the rumors was that John Mathis had witnessed the plane and that's why his family was killed, said Kirkus.

"We were able to dispel that rumor, and there were other rumors about drugs," said Kirkus. "There was nothing we could ever substantiate that John was ever involved in a drug deal."

Chapter 15

REFLECTIONS

Wally Eklund, cocounsel in one of the most infamous murder trials in South Dakota history, is retired and living in Gregory, where he began his legal career in 1971 fresh out of law school. The acquittal of John Mathis lifted the widely recognized Johnson Eklund law firm to even greater heights in the pantheon of South Dakota trial lawyers.

It wasn't all glamour.

"It was a non-stop work project for me from the time we took it on until well after the trial," Eklund, seventy-five, said in January 2021.

Asked if he thought the theory related by jury foreman Honomichl had any merit, Eklund was circumspect.

"Well, it's still a mystery to me. John had indicated that he was confronted outside the metal shed and somebody wrote in spray paint that Mathus sucks and misspelled Mathis, and you're talking about someone with a 65 or 75 IQ, so how would he know to misspell his name?"

Eklund and Johnson had called on Lincoln County state's attorney Jeff Masten as an expert witness. Masten possessed a master's degree in theoretical physics and challenged the FBI's conclusions on the similarities of the spent cartridges and the unspent shell found on John Mathis. Masten said the bullets were similar only because they were manufactured by the same company.

"He took apart the FBI on matching bullets, making them unmatched bullets," Eklund said. "If there was any truth to the allegation that Mathis did that, where the hell is the gun?"

Despite the most thorough search of its day, law enforcement was never able to find the murder weapon. Ballistics tests showing it to be a .22-caliber rifle were not disputed, but the gun itself disappeared and remained a key unanswered question in the decades following the trial. The absence of the gun was a major factor in the acquittal of John Mathis.

A number of guns were discovered and tested over time, and one found in the basement of a Mitchell residence in September 2001 held promise in unraveling the mystery. It was a .22-caliber Marlin semiautomatic, the exact type of gun that was thought to be the murder weapon. According to a report from the Sanborn County Sheriff's Office, Ralph Shawd of Mitchell had contacted authorities and said his grandson had found a rifle in the basement of the home of his deceased father, Perry. What made the discovery even more compelling was that Ralph Shawd said he had met Vern Mathis Jr. at a local gas station two months previously, and Vern Jr. had shared that his father, Vern Sr., was then living at Firesteel Nursing Home. According to Shawd, Vern Jr. added, "You have the rifle," and then he left.[151]

The rifle, a Marlin Model M2 989 with no visible serial number, was sent to the state Department of Criminal Investigation testing laboratory in Pierre by DCI agent Dennis Marek of Mitchell. The test results did not connect the gun to the murders.

Seven years later, law enforcement received not only another lead on the missing gun, but much more.

A nurse's aide at Firesteel Nursing Home in Mitchell said that Vern Mathis Sr. told her he had done something "terrible."[152]

The aide, who had been employed at Firesteel for a year, was working the night shift, and about eleven o'clock at night, she stopped at Vern Mathis's room to check on him. He had been in poor health, according to the aide, and she wanted to see how he was before her duties ended.

Mathis was awake, but groggy, according to an interview later with Sergeant Mike Koster of the Mitchell Police Department. Mathis told the aide that "he had done something terrible. He had helped his son do something terrible."[153]

"He had hidden the gun," according to the aide. Mathis didn't say anything else and just looked away at the wall.[154]

When Mathis told the aide this, she "freaked out" and left the room. She didn't know what Mathis was talking about, so she called her father and told him what Mathis had said, according to the police report.[155]

The aide's father remembered the Mathis murder case and called the Mitchell Police Department.[156] The incident spurred the police and the

Davison County Sheriff's Office to arrange to see Mathis at the nursing home. Sheriff Dave Miles drove to the police department, picked up Detective Toby Russell and proceeded to the nursing home, where they met DCI agent Dennis Marek. A nurse let them in, and they were escorted to the west wing, where Mathis was staying. According to the incident report, Miles and the charge nurse stood in the doorway of Mathis's room while Russell and Marek explained to Mathis why they were there so late and that he did not have to speak to them if he did not want to. Mathis, according to the report, denied knowing anything about a gun or hiding a gun.

Two days later, public safety chief Lyndon Overweg and police lieutenant Don Everson interviewed Mathis in his room.[157]

When Overweg asked Mathis if he knew the whereabouts of the gun used in the incident at the Mathis farm, Mathis replied, "Why?" Then he said he didn't "know a damn thing about it."

Overweg then asked Mathis if Ralph Shawd was involved in the case or if Mathis knew anything about the gun found in Shawd's basement. Mathis replied, "Not that I know of."

When Overweg asked Mathis if it would give him peace to share information about the gun, Mathis indicated he would rather keep the information in. He said that he would rather take the information to his grave.[158]

Overweg pressed on, asking Mathis again where the gun could be found, to which Mathis answered, "Whatever they find out or dug up." Overweg asked Mathis how far down the gun would be buried, but Mathis did not clarify further.

Overweg also asked Mathis if he had information about the case and if he would share it, and Mathis's response was that he did not know if he would share the information.[159]

Toward the end of the interview, Overweg said he "told Vern Sr. that I believed what happened was a choice beyond Vern's, he got caught up in it after it happened. When I asked if this was a true statement, Vern Sr. replied, 'I don't know.'"

Overweg also asked Mathis if he was involved in the planning of the incident. Mathis replied, "There's no way in hell."[160]

The murder weapon aside, the masked man scenario remained puzzling. Even Eklund acknowledged that the motive for the murders was murky. How or why could a masked intruder locate the Mathis shed and kill Ladonna Mathis and her two sons and not John Mathis?

"Crazy things happen in this world," Eklund said. He then related a story about a boy who attended high school with him and was in his wife's class.

"Danny Murphy was a schoolteacher in Brandon. He visited some friends in Connecticut or somewhere and was murdered. He grew up in Winner and just happened to have a friend in the eastern United States and some guy had thought his wife had taken refuge in his friend's house and he murdered Danny. Crazy stuff like that can happen."

Eklund said he had seen Mathis only two or three times in the last forty years.

"He never complained, but he seemed to be a pretty lonely soul," Eklund said.

For those who still doubt that John Mathis deserved acquittal, Eklund said, "I haven't had to debate that with anybody. Nobody has raised that in my presence."

For Holmes, sixty-six, second chair in the state's prosecution of John Mathis, the memory of the case is etched in his mind.

"I don't drive past the Mount Vernon exit without thinking of it," he said in early 2021. "You have cases you work on; it is part of your career. You look at your job as putting evidence before the jury in an ethical and professional manner and arguing the case the best you can and if you've done that, you've done your job. But you can't be human without a personal connection to your case."

Holmes recalled the answer lawyer Lynn Crooks gave to a reporter who asked him to name his greatest trial victory. Crooks, an assistant U.S. attorney in Fargo, North Dakota, had successfully prosecuted Leonard Peltier in 1977 in connection with the murder of two FBI agents.

"The ones you remember most are the ones you lost," Crooks said. "That's true for any trial lawyer."

The missing gun, a .22 caliber, has never been found, and it was a large hurdle for the prosecution to overcome. The search was intense and extensive.

"It wasn't for lack of trying. I have a more experienced perspective now. They [the investigators] did an excellent job. I've known Lyle [Davison County sheriff Lyle Swenson] my whole career. He took it harder than anyone else. Woulda, coulda, shoulda. I tell my young prosecutors all the time, analyze and learn from it, but don't key in on it. You could probably do it on the case where you get the guilty verdict, but you don't do it because you get the result you expected," Holmes said.

Holmes's boss, Mark Meierhenry, always said he lost the case because the jury could not come to grips with the idea that a father could kill his children.

"Some things are black and white, some things aren't. Anytime you get a homicide within a domestic or family relationship it is difficult with juries. Especially with children. Easier for juries to understand with spouses," Holmes said.

Another defense argument was that no fingerprints were taken at the scene. Investigators said too many people had come and gone for fingerprints to be viable. Johnson and Eklund also made the point that the engine in Mathis's pickup wasn't checked for warmth, to see if it had been driven. Those may have been factors in the acquittal, but "you never know," Holmes said. "The conclusion I've gotten, there was a lot less evidence of guilt where we've obtained convictions.

"It's always difficult to know what resonates with a jury. I've talked to juries after the fact when it's fresh in their mind and you don't know if it's their impression or the whole jury of a justification of a decision. They say 'we did this' but it may not be the real reason…that there was more to it."

DCI agent David Muller, in an April 2020 interview, remembers vividly the discussion about checking engines of vehicles at the Mathis place.

"One of the problems we had, three days into the search, a neighbor came up and said, 'I want you to know I've been a neighbor of John Mathis and all of those years his pickup has been backed into the machine shed. Now it is driven into the machine shed. Something is wrong with that.' We didn't know anything about that. Hindsight being 20/20, someone should have checked the engine. That might have taken care of what happened to the gun.

"My theory is that John shot himself, drove someplace and got rid of the gun. The arm was hurting so bad he just drove into the shed."

Muller did most of the work on the crime scene, collecting evidence and taking photographs "before anyone touched anything. Davison County is pretty competent and didn't screw up the crime scene."

A Canton native, Muller began his law enforcement career in Huron after graduating from Huron College. Four-and-a-half years later, he applied to work with the DCI and was working security for the state fair in Huron when the call came about the Mathis murders.

When he arrived on the scene, he thought, "This is going to be a mess."

"I had worked several homicides. They are all a little bit different. I would not say it was any better or any worse, other than a couple of kids and the mother were killed. They were shot in bed and that made it a little different. Normally, you don't have young children as victims in the homicide scene."

Muller said the next step was to go through and take a close look at the scene. There were .22-caliber rounds scattered around the inside of the machine shed.

"Lyle and I talked about checking for fingerprints and decided it would be a waste of time since there had been a number of people in and out of the entrance door. Normally you'd brush for fingerprints. It looks good on TV.

Rick Johnson shoved that up our ass big time at trial. At pretrial, he asked if anyone had checked for fingerprints. He said, 'Oh, juries like fingerprints,' so I knew we were in trouble from the get-go."

"You'd have to see the crime scene. Nothing to check. Hindsight is 20/20. I could have spread some fingerprint powder around just to say I'd done it, because that was the first question Rick asked," Muller said.

"The only thing you can say is that fingerprints are overrated. It's kind of ironic, because my daughter in the DCI lab checks for fingerprints. She says when she testifies in court, the first half of her testimony is, 'Don't believe what you see on TV because this isn't how the world works.'"

The search for evidence, including the missing gun, took twenty days, "maybe longer."

"We had people come out—Lyle put out the call to other agencies—and we walked through the place. The land area was pretty good sized, in the neighborhood of a quarter of a section. We interviewed all the neighbors around there, trying to get some feel of what was going on at the Mathis place," Muller said.

"We interviewed Vern and Vern Jr., and the impression was that he [John Mathis] was a strange duck, didn't socialize with anyone in the area.

"You talk to everybody and try to figure out what happened, that's all you can do. You can sum it up in five minutes; several days and weeks will get you that five minutes."

Muller said he was surprised by the acquittal: "I didn't figure there was any way a jury would let him go."

That view was shared by the court reporter, Gary Lutgen, in spite of his high regard for the defense team, Rick Johnson in particular.

Lutgen, who attended junior college in Mason City, Iowa, and played football there, didn't take the academic side seriously. His dad told him he would no longer underwrite his college education, so Lutgen, after learning from a cousin that court reporting school might be a good career choice, moved to Minneapolis and enrolled at the Minnesota School of Business. He landed his first position in Mankato, Minnesota, then a second job in Lyman County, South Dakota, working for Judge John Jones. Jones would later become a federal judge in Sioux Falls, but Lutgen didn't wait for that, taking the court reporting job with Anderst instead.

"I always liked Tom. He was a fair judge and did a good job. He was a hard worker. He wasn't real strict and he was patient and smart. He handled the courtroom well and I think everyone respected him," Lutgen said in a January 2021 interview.

Court reporter Gary Lutgen.
Lutgen collection.

During the time Lutgen worked with Anderst, the Mathis trial was "the worst one I had to sit through, and for him, too."

The fact that a wife and two children were shot while sleeping, and there were pictures of them in pools of blood, was almost too much for Lutgen, who had children about the same age as the two Mathis boys.

"I saw my judge cry and I saw every juror cry at one time and I know I did. It was hard to hear over and over."

Lutgen thought the investigation was thorough, from the pumping of the hog manure pits to walking the cornfields. "Those guys didn't miss a spot."

Like many other courtroom observers, Lutgen theorized that the gun had been removed from the scene and the farm. "There's no way the killer could have hidden it," he said.

John Mathis was a man under a lot of stress, Lutgen said: living in a machine shed, no running water, no toilets, building a new house. "I don't think it was all roses in the marital home."

"I don't know how any father/husband could go through that without breaking down. There was one point he was on the stand, explaining how it happened. When he did that yell, it caught me by surprise and the gal writing for the newspaper wrote the next day that the court reporter blanched. I about came out of my chair. I kidded her about it the next day."

Lutgen wonders to this day why a masked intruder, after going to the trouble of killing a woman and two children, would leave a witness.

"That's preposterous," he said.

Perhaps.

But not to Duane Mathis, now recently turned forty, who maintains his father's innocence.

Over the many decades since the trial, both John Mathis and his son have stood their ground, defending the Yankton jury's acquittal.

The media coverage was unfair, Duane said in early 2021. His remarks dovetail with public opinion polls today concerning the media.

"It was one-sided," said Duane, when asked what he didn't like about the coverage of his dad's trial. "You know, it was like, hurry up and point a finger and be done."

Ten years earlier, Duane drove to Mitchell and walked into the office of the *Daily Republic* in order to prove to the reporter that he was who he said he was over the telephone.

Then he said his dad had not committed the heinous crime.

"I don't believe he did it," said Duane, then thirty. "If he had, I wouldn't be here."

After the acquittal, John Mathis drove to the home of his late wife's parents, Lorenz and Evelyn Gerlach, collected his infant son and took him home.

John raised him and, during that time, sometimes talked about the early years.

"We talked in bits and pieces," Duane said of his conversations with his dad. "We never sat down and talked about it. He doesn't relive the situation."

Duane said he reconnected with his mother's family in later years, "when I was older, a few years ago." But he doesn't visit other family members, saying simply, "If you ask me about my relatives, I wouldn't know. I never kept up on it."

Duane and his girlfriend of eleven years live on the Mathis place with their three sons. The land is gone, a victim of the agriculture washout of the 1980s and 1990s, he said. "Cattle and pigs went down. They had to sell out."

He believes if the crime occurred today, better information would have bolstered his dad's case. "With today's technology, I think it would be different, with DNA testing and all the stuff they do now."

A decade earlier, Duane said, "You've got to know the person before you actually accuse them."

He stands by that statement today.

Passage of time has largely limited the media's retrospective of the case. The reporter who covered the trial for the *Yankton Press & Dakotan*, Jim Van Osdel, eighty-two, remembers that the Mathis defense team showed exceptional ability.

"Suffice it to say that Eklund and Johnson did a marvelous job of representing their client. Masterful.

"There was no evidence that he [Mathis] did it. And [Mark] Meierhenry didn't provide any evidence that he did do it," Van Osdel said.

Jerry Oster, news director of WNAX radio in Yankton, remembers covering the trial on days when certain witnesses were to testify or crucial evidence was to be presented.

"It was huge news," said Oster in a January 2021 interview. Oster, sixty-seven, who has been with WNAX since 1976, said the importance of the case was reflected in one way by the choice of legal counsel.

Former Davison County sheriff Lyle Swenson in 2020, at his office in the Carnegie Resource Center in Mitchell. *Author's photo.*

"Attorney General Mark Meierhenry and Rick Johnson, one of the best hired guns around. High profile. From what I saw, Meierhenry was pretty cool and collected and Rick was a little more dramatic, at times."

Oster pointed out that the state always had the bigger burden, while the defense team's job was to deflect and defend, leaving questions in the jurors' minds, if possible.

"In talking to jurors later, the prosecution opened the door and never walked through. I think they were ready to convict but never got that clear path."

Many of the jurors were staying in the same motel, and Oster would go over and "hang out and just listen."

Was he surprised by the acquittal? "Kind of. I think the expectation was he'd be found guilty and when he wasn't, it surprised people. I try to keep an open mind about it. I think the prosecution thought they had it won, but they didn't push them through the door. Maybe it was because of the kids."

David Kranz, the reporter for the *Daily Republic*, covered the trial and the story. He died in June 2018. The *Argus Leader* reporter who covered the trial was unavailable for an interview.

Just four months before his death in July 2020, Mark Meierhenry reflected on what he called a positive aspect of the trial. After John Mathis was acquitted, Meierhenry was discussing the verdict with Bill Janklow, his friend and the governor of South Dakota at the time. One topic that came up was mandatory reporting of child abuse.

"Bill jumped in with the power of the governor's office and we said we were going to work together to get the legislature to pass what we now have, and we were one of the first states. It was extensive. Teachers and doctors were against it, anyone who had to report it, but it passed.

"If he [Mathis] had been convicted, we would have been one of the last states instead of one of the first states requiring mandatory reporting.

"That to me is part of the story."

INTERVIEWS

Eklund, Wally, December 11, 2020.
Gerlach, Dwight, February 12, 2021.
Holmes, Dennis, January 7, 2021.
Honomichl, Dianne, December 16, 2020.
Kaemingk, Dennis, November 20, 2020.
Kirkus, Douglas, April 8, 2020.
Lutgen, Gary, January 13, 2021.
Mathis, Duane, January 19, 2021.
Mathis, John, October 20, 2020.
Meierhenry, Mark, March 20, 2020.
Muller, David, April 10, 2020.
Mulloy, Tim, January 14, 2021.
Oster, Jerry, January 28, 2021.
Pochop, Stephanie, January 13, 2021.
Randall, Dr. Brad, February 1, 2021.
Reimnitz, Lyle, January 11, 2021.
Reimnitz, Marilyn, October 29, 2020.
Swenson, Lyle, March 8, 2020.
Van Osdel, Jim, January 14, 2021.
Volk, David, December 14, 2020.

NOTES

Chapter 1

1. Doug Kirkus deposition, December 22, 1981.
2. Ibid.
3. Ibid.
4. Davison County Sheriff's Department case report, September 8, 1981.
5. Doug Kirkus deposition, December 22, 1981.

Chapter 2

6. *Daily Republic*, September 9, 1981.
7. Department of Criminal Investigation report, South Dakota, September 8, 1981.
8. Ibid.
9. *Argus Leader*, September 9, 1981.
10. *Daily Republic*, September 10, 1981.
11. *Argus Leader*, September 12, 1981.
12. *Daily Republic*, September 23, 1981.
13. Associated Press, September 26, 1981.
14. Ibid.
15. *Argus Leader*, September 27, 1981.

Chapter 3

16. *Daily Republic*, October 14, 1981.
17. *Daily Republic*, October 30, 1981.
18. Ibid.
19. *Argus Leader*, October 31, 1981.
20. *Daily Republic*, November 4, 1981.
21. *Daily Republic*, December 10, 1981.
22. *Argus Leader*, January 17, 1982.
23. *Argus Leader*, January 18, 1982.
24. *Daily Republic*, February 26, 1982.
25. Ibid.

Chapter 4

26. *Argus Leader*, April 11, 1982.
27. DCI report, September 12, 1981.
28. Ibid.
29. DCI report, September 30, 1981.
30. Davison County Sheriff's Department case file report.

Chapter 5

31. *Argus Leader*, April 11, 1982.
32. KELO-TV, July 31, 2020.
33. KELO-TV, July 30, 2020.
34. *Argus Leader*, April 11, 1982
35. Ibid.

Chapter 6

36. *Yankton Press & Dakotan*, April 13, 1982.
37. *Daily Republic*, April 12, 1982.
38. Ibid.
39. Ibid.
40. *Argus Leader*, April 13, 1982.
41. *Daily Republic*, April 13, 1982.
42. *Daily Republic*, April 14, 1982.
43. *Argus Leader*, April 15, 1982.
44. Ibid.

45. *Argus Leader*, April 14, 1982.
46. Ibid.
47. *Argus Leader*, April 16, 1982.
48. *Argus Leader*, April 20, 1982.
49. *Daily Republic*, April 20, 1982.
50. Ibid.
51. *Yankton Press & Dakotan*, April 21, 1982.
52. Ibid.
53. Ibid.
54. Ibid.
55. *Daily Republic*, April 21, 1982.
56. Ibid.
57. Ibid.
58. *Argus Leader*, April 23, 1982.

Chapter 7

59. *Daily Republic*, April 22, 1982.
60. *Argus Leader*, April 23, 1982.
61. Ibid.
62. Ibid.
63. Ibid.
64. *Yankton Press & Dakotan*, April 22, 1982.
65. *Daily Republic*, April 23, 1982.
66. Ibid.
67. *Yankton Press & Dakotan*, April 24, 1982.
68. Associated Press, *Daily Republic*, April 26, 1982.
69. *Argus Leader*, April 27, 1982.
70. Ibid.
71. *Daily Republic*, April 26, 1982.
72. *Argus Leader*, April 28, 1982.
73. Ibid.
74. Ibid.
75. Ibid.
76. *Yankton Press & Dakotan*, April 29, 1982.
77. *Daily Republic*, April 28, 1982.
78. *Daily Republic*, April 29, 1982.

Chapter 8

79. Davison County Sheriff's Department case file.
80. Department of Criminal Investigation interview, September 10, 1981.
81. Ibid.
82. *Daily Republic*, April 30, 1982.
83. *Argus Leader*, April 30, 1982.
84. *Daily Republic*, April 30, 1982.
85. Ibid.
86. *Yankton Press & Dakotan*, April 30, 1982.
87. *Argus Leader*, April 30, 1982.
88. Ibid.
89. *Daily Republic*, April 30, 1982.
90. *Yankton Press & Dakotan*, May 1, 1982.
91. *Argus Leader*, May 2, 1982.
92. Ibid.

Chapter 9

93. *Daily Republic*, April 28, 1982.
94. Davison County Sheriff's Department report, October 31, 1981.

Chapter 10

95. *Daily Republic*, May 3, 1982.
96. Ibid.
97. Ibid.
98. *Argus Leader*, May 4, 1982.
99. Ibid.
100. Ibid.
101. *Yankton Press & Dakotan*, May 4, 1982.
102. Ibid.
103. Ibid.
104. *Daily Republic*, May 4, 1982.
105. Ibid.
106. *Daily Republic*, May 5, 1982.
107. *Yankton Press & Dakotan*, May 6, 1982.
108. *Argus Leader*, May 6, 1982.
109. Ibid.
110. Ibid.

111. *Daily Republic*, May 6, 1982.
112. *Argus Leader*, May 6, 1982.
113. *Yankton Press & Dakotan*, May 7, 1982.
114. *Argus Leader*, May 7, 1982.
115. *Daily Republic*, May 7, 1982.
116. Ibid.
117. Ibid.
118. *Daily Republic*, May 8, 1982.

Chapter 11

119. *Daily Republic*, May 10, 1983.
120. Ibid.
121. *Yankton Press & Dakotan*, May 11, 1982.
122. *Daily Republic*, May 11, 1982.
123. *Yankton Press & Dakotan*, May 11, 1982.
124. *Daily Republic*, May 11, 1982.
125. Ibid.
126. Ibid.

Chapter 12

127. *Argus Leader*, May 11, 1982.
128. Ibid.
129. Ibid.
130. *Yankton Press & Dakotan*, May 13, 1982.
131. Ibid.
132. *Daily Republic*, May 13, 1982.
133. Ibid.
134. *Argus Leader*, May 11, 1982.
135. *Yankton Press & Dakotan*, May 11, 1982.
136. *Argus Leader*, May 13, 1982.
137. Ibid.
138. Ibid.
139. *Daily Republic*, May 13, 1982.
140. *Argus Leader*, May 14, 1982.
141. Ibid.
142. Ibid.
143. Ibid.

Chapter 13

144. *Daily Republic*, May 12, 1982.
145. Ibid.
146. Ibid.

Chapter 14

147. *Daily Republic*, September 25, 2007.
148. *Argus Leader*, January 13, 1982.
149. *Daily Republic*, May 6, 1982.
150. Associated Press, *Daily Republic*, January 21, 2005.

Chapter 15

151. Sanborn County Sheriff's Department incident report, September 24, 2001.
152. Mitchell Police Department incident report, March 16, 2008.
153. Ibid.
154. Ibid.
155. Ibid.
156. Ibid.
157. Mitchell Police Department incident report, March 18, 2008.
158. Ibid.
159. Ibid.
160. Ibid.

INDEX

A

Allison, Dorothy 24, 25, 96, 101
Anderst, Thomas 11, 28, 29, 30, 32, 46, 47, 48, 49, 52, 77, 87, 95, 111, 112
Argus Leader 25, 46, 87, 88, 94, 104, 114

B

Baas, Dr. Walter 56
Bittner, George 21, 43, 52
Blackburn, John 43

C

Christenson, Bernie 56, 64

D

Daily Republic 18, 81, 84, 90, 95, 96, 113, 114
Dillon, John, Jr. 61

E

Eklund, Wally 25, 26, 28, 29, 30, 31, 35, 40, 41, 42, 49, 51, 52, 53, 55, 56, 61, 73, 74, 75, 78, 81, 84, 86, 89, 106, 108, 109, 110, 114, 117
Erickson, Deanna 50, 88, 92

G

Gerlach, Dwight 37, 69, 70, 71
Gerlach, Evelyn 29, 35, 37, 68, 71, 95, 96, 113
Gerlach, Lorenz 29, 35, 37, 71, 95, 96, 113
Giegling, Ken 19, 20, 26, 35, 58, 65, 66
Gienapp, David 40, 41
Greibel, Pete 90

H

Hanson, Cliff 50

Index

Harris, Ray 49, 50, 92
Haugen, Burnell 50, 91, 92
Holmes, Dennis 41, 44, 45, 77, 78, 81, 86, 88, 102, 109, 110, 117
Honomichl, Dianne 104
Honomichl, Gary 50, 88, 91, 92, 95, 96, 103, 104, 106, 117

J

Jackley, Marty 45
Janklow, Bill 31, 40, 43, 115
Janklow, Russell 43
Johnson, Rick 11, 30, 31, 32, 35, 36, 39, 40, 41, 42, 43, 45, 46, 47, 48, 49, 52, 55, 56, 61, 67, 68, 73, 81, 84, 85, 88, 89, 94, 101, 106, 110, 111, 114

K

Kaemingk, Dennis 63, 64, 117
Kiner, Patrick 22, 25, 73, 77, 88
King, Jane 88, 92
Kirkus, Doug 7, 13, 14, 15, 16, 17, 18, 19, 20, 26, 28, 34, 35, 51, 52, 54, 55, 56, 58, 61, 65, 73, 75, 76, 94, 96, 101, 102, 105, 117

L

Lutgen, Gary 75, 111, 112, 113, 117

M

MacDonell, Herbert 77, 78
Masten, Jeff 79, 106
Mathis, Duane 97, 113

Mathis, John 11, 13, 15, 16, 18, 22, 25, 26, 28, 29, 30, 31, 32, 33, 35, 39, 46, 49, 50, 51, 54, 58, 59, 62, 64, 66, 68, 71, 73, 74, 76, 77, 78, 79, 80, 81, 82, 83, 84, 85, 88, 91, 93, 95, 96, 98, 101, 102, 103, 104, 105, 106, 107, 108, 109, 110, 112, 113, 115
Mathis, Ladonna 9, 11, 16, 17, 20, 22, 24, 25, 29, 33, 35, 37, 46, 50, 51, 58, 60, 61, 65, 66, 68, 69, 70, 71, 74, 75, 76, 77, 78, 81, 84, 85, 86, 91, 93, 95, 98, 101, 102, 108
Mathis, Vern 15, 16, 18, 35, 41, 58, 59, 69, 75, 107
Meierhenry, Mark 11, 25, 26, 28, 29, 30, 31, 32, 39, 40, 41, 42, 43, 44, 45, 46, 47, 48, 49, 50, 52, 53, 55, 56, 57, 58, 59, 61, 65, 67, 68, 74, 76, 77, 78, 79, 81, 82, 83, 84, 85, 86, 87, 89, 93, 97, 98, 99, 101, 102, 104, 105, 109, 114, 115, 117
Miller, Dr. Frederick 79
Miller, Walter 67
Moline, Kim 96
Mount Vernon 10, 13, 14, 22, 25, 26, 30, 33, 34, 37, 52, 76, 89, 90, 109
Muller, David 35, 58, 110, 111, 117
Mulloy, Tim 77, 78, 80, 94, 95, 104, 105, 117

Index

O

Oster, Jerry 114, 117

P

Pankratz, Lorin 65
Peele, Ernest 61

R

Randall, Dr. Brad 9, 59, 60, 61, 117
Reimnitz, Lyle 35, 37, 71
Reimnitz, Marilyn 35, 70
Roesler, Eugene 22, 33

S

Sargent, Clint 42, 43
Seiler, Randy 45
Swenson, Lyle 7, 18, 19, 22, 24, 25, 28, 31, 34, 35, 56, 57, 59, 64, 71, 89, 94, 95, 96, 101, 109, 117

T

Tatum, Bonnie 51, 66
Tatum, Kim 29, 30, 44, 51, 58, 65, 67, 68, 76, 80, 82, 84, 92
Thompson, Charles 40, 41, 42

V

Van Osdel, Jim 114, 117
Volk, David 39, 44, 117

W

Wieczorek, Donna 56
Wraxall, Brian 78

Y

Yankton Press & Dakotan 114

Z

Zeldes, Elya 61

ABOUT THE AUTHOR

South Dakota native Noel Hamiel is a career journalist who retired in 2007, then spent five years traveling the state for the South Dakota Community Foundation, helping communities establish their own philanthropic funds. His first book, *Sketches of South Dakota*, was published in 2001. A former state legislator, he was inducted into the South Dakota Newspaper Hall of Fame in 2012. He and his wife, Janet, live in Rapid City and have three grown daughters and ten grandchildren.

CPSIA information can be obtained
at www.ICGtesting.com
Printed in the USA

AVENUE OF PURPOSE

Using Finance To Point You To Your Purpose

Betina McCadney

ation may be reproduced, distributed,
ny means, including photocopying,
hanical methods, without the prior
ccept in the case of brief quotations
ertain other noncommercial uses
sion requests, write to the publisher,
dinator," at info@beyondpublishing.

available on quantity purchases by
For details, contact the publisher at

olesalers. Email info@

can bring authors to your live event.
vent contact the Beyond Publishing
ing.net

eyondPublishing.net

ited States of America distributed

ey

THE POWI
OF PC

Have you ever found yourself in

- Have you been denied a m
- Have you needed to purch
  to the dealership to buy th
  end up leaving with nothi
  but hated?
- Have you had a medical en
  for your excruciating pai
  once doing so, being treat
  lack thereof afforded you?
- Have you needed dental c
  treatment for fear of the bi

Then you, My Friend, hav poverty. Many people easily eq you earn or have access to. But how you're treated in the world Think trumped-up charges, you you did not do and the options different between a paid attorn client and a public defender that coercing you into taking a deal.

can literally change a person's
talking to a friend who is now
Unfortunately, many of her beliefs
from the damaging treatment she
poor and in need of emergency
r and business coach, she is a
many times, the fear of healthcare
owerless like the teenage girl that
because she had state-funded
ness was bred in mistrust from
ed at the hands of professionals
t at heart and did not. And when
ous prices for that powerlessness,

s like a tertiary wound bleeding
hen you're worried about money,
houghts of lack creep into what
e night terrors. Then because
you are sluggish in the morning.
that you now have to go to a job
you give your all, it doesn't pay
That irritation travels with you
he person who cut you off as you
parking space even close to the
inger out on your steering wheel
g. After finding a parking spot
e time you're supposed to clock

in. Now you're nearly in tears
boss's comment about you be
some hateful force, that migr
have checked out starts creep
possible today.

Poverty can make your
hellish Groundhog Days loop
dastardly existence too painfu
too well. At some point, you'
accept mere existence. At sor
poverty is a choice. And jus
something else. If you're read
to change your financial life
for you.

TABLE OF

SECTION 1

Chapter	1	Introduction
Chapter	2	Growing Up
Chapter	3	Snake Eyes
Chapter	4	Good Job, Poor Li
Chapter	5	The Definition
Chapter	6	Financial Coachin
Chapter	7	Rear-View Mirror
Chapter	8	Roadmap to Purp

SECTION 2

Chapter 9

SECTION 3

Chapter 10 How to make a rig
Avenue of Purpos

SE

COA
THE

CHA[

INTROD[

I'm a bit of a dreamer, bu[
life I have now and I'm still reach[
I've dreamed of things: houses, c[
thought was a good life, I did not [
of the true fulfillment of financ[
These are the things that Purpose[

Before getting on my path [
dreams, I lived like many people [
lot worse. As a single mom with [
most of the time. Even when I [
decent money, I still had no m[
income increase, so much of the [
or another. I may as well have [
two weeks into a purse with a h[
principles. I've been evicted, had [
unit. Name a financial issue and [
it. I am writing this book becaus[

successful you'll be, it's how you

d South Central Los Angeles. Like ny neighborhood, we survived on l standards, we were poor, but we our house was clean, and because :r, food was in abundance. I don't until I reached junior high school). It was then that the distinction e way teenagers dressed. At this and I did not want that to be my problem was that I did not know oung adult, I was mirroring the s around me make. It took a life- wakening for me to realize I was needed to make a change. From ng how to do money right.

a very successful company with e car of my dreams. I live in the r YEARS, with shade trees, peace, rry when using my cards whether r pay my bills in part. I no longer nds and loved ones. I no longer l of that, I am debt-free and I've my adult children. At this point, can improve their financial life

experience. I'm talking privat no one in my family has seen

I said all this not to br I've had to overcome in hopes Purpose and living the life of a monetizable purpose that is overflow in our lives. I believe overcome are not for us. We a path for those who follow u journey of life a little easier. He knew our beginning fron through the trials and would is in the thick of it.

I now live a life of ser helped my kids, my family, an my path and found my Avenu financially stable and use my helped you. But I certainly c;

You too can find your take a shortcut. My road wa that does not have to be your know the way and can lead yo help you discard your limitin who you are and what you we dirt and grime out of the way the end of the tunnel. You

...ul and more confident in your ... more productive because you ... r person overall.

...pture is 2 Kings 4:1-7 the story ...s. Paraphrased: The widow's ...try. He died in debt. Now we ...d with money, overborrowed, ...de clear through this passage. ...people and the creditors came ...o sons into slavery as payment

...lisha for help. Elisha did not ... What he asked her was what ...ot anything in the house, save ...her response was her ability ...bout that later). Many of my ...se (her used interchangeably ...y they, many times, have not ... For years I was locked in an ...otion was often destroyed by ...eep me from promoting and ...my output, education, and my ...osition.

...ed to go abroad and borrow ...n she and her children were ...he door and pour the oil until ...the oil would not stay until all the jars were full. They did as the... the vessels, went into their hom... flowed until there were no mor... stopped just as the prophet Elis... of instruction was fulfilled, the... needing to know what to do next...

This portion of the passage... the foundation for my company... show you is you have at least on... flow and provide wealth for you... have to first be willing to fill vess... community) with those gifts and ... happens.

The reason the prophet Elis... and foundational to me is becau... this story with revelation.

Elisha's second set of inst... simple:

1. Go
2. Sell the oil
3. Pay your debts
4. And you and your child...

ction. Many times, we are in a
ning that it becomes debilitating.
e, we stop wanting to feel what is
angst. Maybe the widow woman
 action and out of the place of

ave a purpose that is monetizable.
to many people but for me, there
of you that is meant to be used in

ewardship. If you've heard me
 I've written, it usually leads to
ship Activates Purpose. When
of bills being paid, having saved
 having invested for your future,
, and you have some money left
eed…that is the best place from
or existence either for yourself or
 inspiration from all things being

off the rest says to me that the
 not going to create just enough
low. Your purpose will take you

You are not meant to stru
But it is not your portion. It
ourselves, our capabilities, o
future. Because so much of
struggle, it becomes our realit
all our strength against to see

Notice I capitalize Purpo
an extension of you. Like wh
the first letter. You see it as
to realize. The part of you tha
in the style you do and with
an entire community of peop
what you have to offer.

Purpose is your undenia
becomes the very definition
of what you're most passiona
for you, it did not start out as
Purpose started as your greate
was going to turn that very t
My personal example of that
doing all that I could to impa
abruptly thrust into entrepren
That fizzled out rather quickl
in dentistry was my meantim
provision while I was being r
author, the business owner, a
having previously thought ab

through can be used to help

beginning of my life seemed
Like many today, I overlooked
ed by my circumstances and
e wrong path and hit a dead
ded to make a U-turn to find

uld be dirty and grungy. Just
to do. It operates as the deep
to let you know that there is
you have a responsibility to
ds and it provides enough for
ive in abundance. Here's my

CHAF

GROW

Recently I began seeing a
was necessary. I believe you n
or the other. In my first appointr
the therapist just wanted the fact
to be. She asked how my parents
mom (looking for an escape fro
met my dad the day he was releas
and saw an easy target in her. L
mother looking for love and a fat
knocked him upside the head." T

While my dad was continu
mom was having three more ch
I was growing. I was growing in
child. Soon, I became the mothe
young, single mother was always
doing what she could to work to
best she could with no education

n, welfare was the only consistent
ln't stretch far.

in our household were limited
people that grew up in similar
that list:

on't ask for NUTHIN'!

hrough the eye of a needle, than
o heaven

community were justifying being
icrasies. What I later learned, is
gative beliefs about money were
parents or caregivers and even

a mother, repeating the cycles I
that, I was a statistic. I had been
id cleaning after kids for so long
ige, I answered the call with wild
out money, we also didn't discuss
is is a whole other book in another
over the next 4 years and found
ie exact same life my mother had
was I had not suffered her kinds
l therefore, had no need to self-
; a right mind, I decided to reject

what to me appeared as settl:
I thought I was better than m
and to me, she was just silly ar
mother. While I wasn't sure w
looked like, I knew what I'd se
food stamps -were all things
decision alone made me bett
was going to have a better life
the hood. I was not going to
were going to have opportur
than my mother, my aunts, a
had limited opportunities anc
it. I was going to make my m;
reflected that.

It would happen. Just n

CHA[P]

SNAK[E]

Lack of money leads to d[o] prison. At 23-years-old I was a[n] adult decisions and choices. I [h] my kids ate well because if I did to cook and clean. What I did n[ot] keeping money. I worked a dead-[end] the time I did not even have the v[ision] with growth potential. Meanwhi[le] dad was married to someone els[e] time, I had developed an affinit[y] In short, I was materialistic but [no] checkbook.

I was desperate for stabilit[y] slightest idea how to achieve that me successfully committing crim[e] eldest sibling, every time my yo[ung]

...usand dollars at a time. The issue ...behind, that the money would be ...s if I was caught in this cycle of ...ve forward.

...l education, inconsistent familial ...g desire to finally get ahead and ...gly always pending eviction or ...d get it myself. I wasn't going to ...eone else's table. Instead, I was ...n the primary focus of supporting ...d I be in a position to help others

...tions I could see involved me ...reserver I saw, was linked to a ...ht, I searched myself for options ...ade phone calls, reaching out to ...ange my abysmal circumstances, ...oor choices up to that point the

...begging and pleading, taking five ...found my resolve and decided to ..., lose or draw I was not going to ...oll the dice in a life of crime and

...a major department store during ...ow the Brinks truck kept missing

their pick-ups. The first time... perked up. We hung out so... conversation. By the time sh... begun devising a plan to rob... people I knew that had com... more intimately familiar with... touch it. Too soon. Not enou... I could pull this off.

With the inside help o... another friend, I took the big... roller's table of life gambling... money that wasn't mine. I f... corporation. I felt superior t... theft. If I was gonna go bad, I... myself, that I had thought o... with this major crime. Not l... entered my thought process. ... muster, I rolled the dice of ch...

For the first and only t... moment, everything I had ju... of my beautiful children. My... was always so attentive and p... SHAME. Oh, the shame! B... subsequent arrest were ever... KNEW. While no one was ... of the crime, I was about to ... criminal.

.s given prison time. 9 years to
serve due to the violence and
physically but it was an armed

had broken the law. I wasn't
d to my slap on the wrist? I
well-spoken. I have a pretty
an be somebody! None of that
at I am nothing but a common

ve been so stupid? How could
ln't deserve this. I knew I was
eant. Once I was able to clear
p. What I wasn't going to do
ad, I would do my life's work.
elf-help books and the Oprah
I began by asking myself why
looking for love in a man that
did I find myself in the exact
I vehemently rejected when
ad sense enough to never get

wisely. I tapped into myself.
education, a career, to never
just wanted a life that looked
iving. I was in prison but I

refused to be imprisoned in my
that mindset of programming. I
of freedom and never looked bac

The Coach

As a Certified Financial an
I was experiencing was Cognitiv
author Dan Heath dedicates an
state. Tunneling is what happen
experience extreme poverty or
mental bandwidth suffers to the
problems to overshadow the big
daily. Research shows, that we do
of our problems becomes too r
them all out and develop tunnel
two. The issue with this is that tl
the problems in one way or ano
financial decisions according to
describe was exactly my experien
thinking, and less in charge. As

as it sounds, it literally nev
caught. I just could not process
too intent on solving the financ
the hardest. It became impossi
negative outcome. What ultima
of my actions that day for me

paper. I was given the time to
and get off the crime train with

C H

GOOD JOE

Fast forward to my rele
my life deconstructing and r
thought I knew. Now it's tim
not how you start it's how yo
my personal development jou
I could get my hands on. I n
broken relationships between
provide for them. This was no

I hit the ground runnin
was driven. I had something t
after having been introduced t
and a sheer will to be free, I ed
love for the industry into a 2
a lot of money. After two o
around and positioning mysel
industry, I honed my skill wh

, I was making more money
in varying fields. Not having
t made me desperate in the
. Once free, I was focused on
izable skills - I was doing well
ot have the financial acumen
ch my income. There were
degree that I would consider
efinitely struggles.

ls having a better upbringing
100d". My thinking was that
ings, where crime wasn't so
hat as an option when things
yone.

ecent enough salary to afford
children. But and here's the
nately, I was still stuck in the
level. This is where chasing
norance, I began demanding
rs. This became a running
did, throughout my career, I
nore than anyone else in my
s justified by my output and
ll lived like a pauper. My kids
familiar? The utilities were
y needed and most of what
ED OUT about our financial

situation. I couldn't save. An em
unicorn I could never fully gras;
to send them to college was as in
open. Just never going to happen

The Coach

What I now know is that
struggle/poverty. It wasn't until
human behavior surrounding fin;
I learned about the Psycho-Cyber
thermostat at different times in t
recognize your setting. Because
change my financial thermostat
if I was given a million tax-free
short time.

C H

THE D

The reason many of you
is that it is relatively new. It wa
– "steering your mind to a p
the greatest port in the world,
positive look at this mechani
see the thermostat is neutral
An example of this is the "L
Business Insider called "20 L
few of the examples in this a
same topic seem to point the
is inherently bad. But I've n
anyone to put it in a slot mac

Many of the examples a
you cannot see yourself as a
given that amount of money,
back to the financial status

1at is the set of circumstances
urvive, they've had to do that
ely different conversation and
. Thriving, while a good thing
 had all my life. It puts me in
et of problems like setting up
lone. "Nah", (subconsciously)
ids I know, with the problems
iy struggle what would I talk

f people understanding their
le is credit. Roughly 50% of
es. Many of them believe that
, they would do better with a

g citing that 8% of bankruptcy
seem like a lot of people. To
fornia alone, 240,151 people
2 of those same people found
second time and filed again.
of having to file the first time
etimes they don't go as far as
e. They just find themselves
We've all found ourselves in
u get me outta this…" and in
our bargaining session with
tat that needs calibration.

The Coach

As you can see, having a
Learning new financial tools and
money makes Tunneling less of
plans, options, and an emergenc
my babies were home. Whew!
saved me so much time, energy,
much of their childhood bouncin
frustrated. Grateful that I had a
love on them and teach them wh
frustrated that I still had a slightl
problems that took me from then

In the first couple of years
Umbrella Financial requesting cr
to assess their financial acumen I'd
I would complete the service, se
life, and sometimes in just a few
way back to a low credit score. I
So much so that I would charg
time around. It wasn't until I beg
happening that I realized that ne
symptom. If I was going to help
to have to help them maintain t
take more than just the practical
on that mindset.

C H

FINANCI

Oh, now you're teachin

Yes.

I.

Am.

I went on a journey to
that just weren't available to n
We were all pretty much l
existence. We were all strug
this, my company earns ten
we're on par to earn seven fig
HUGE considering I could n
account when I was in my m
mindset and began to unders

So how did I go from l
business earning $100k a mor
entrepreneur? Well, it started

n to the bank near her home. haw Boulevard when the light from the brake to the gas, the ear-ending my car. I was hurt. ver having been off work, not ny good-paying job every day,

at accident, I was on the 405 ock. There was a motorcyclist mirror to see this freight truck n hit the year before, I began like he was slowing down. I e's gonna hit me." Pushing on a hit Me!" Turning my wheel or unsuspecting motorcyclist, mpact. Airbags deployed. The Mustang. His bike was on its n his phone too late to prevent d out of the car first to check e was, just shaken up. I then reight truck driver about how cycle rider. In my anger, I did sition I was risking my life as nal, high-speed pace. I stood and said to God, "Okay Sir, iously you want my attention. at that moment what I felt in

my spirit was, "Sit down". I did. I body was hurt ten times worse w

Doctors took me off work f into a year due to the progress home, many of my dentist clients clarity, and instructions on how while at work. Many of them en your own business. No one can c entrepreneurship before. I neve myself leading in this way. I neve was a worker bee, or so I though

After hearing that stateme different dental professionals, I Natural Beauty Dental Studio wa credit and my savings. This was was great. I had never before tapp skills without being led by anot but short-lived. Just a few short I had to close the doors of my de wonderful paying clients, or a g because I did not know the busir the time to learn about and un Instead, I used my personal cred personal credit cards to float the That high utilization destroyed n did not have the wherewithal to

ough to profitability. I did not
t me greatly.

auty was a personal sonic boom!
learned nothing else in my life
vork, I learned to fail forward. I
n in every situation I find myself
to teach me".

devastation of having to close
nt of a "failed" venture, and the
ny old career, I once again got to
d what I did not know, I wanted
ne more business owner would
ack of access to working capital
mbrella Financial, Inc was born.
y to begin yet another business,
done better with Natural Beauty.
ch and study, I understood and
egan to expand the vision to not
dit-challenged individuals.

y new industry now. I launched.
g on my debt from my previous
le around me, starting with my
ecome the example of a wealth
e around me, have hundreds of
age this and teach it throughout

Now, we have helped
financial acumen. I pride my
free individuals, families, and
their financial life experiences

Credit repair is going w
clients changed as a result of n
to think, what if we could help
altogether? What if Financia
lower-income communities, th
money and begin operating in
their need for the welfare sy
repair altogether? These were
on financial coaching. This is
still dropping regularly.

In coaching my many cl
magnificent blessing to my clie
and monetize their gifts.

Here's what that looks
repair (the symptom). A large
get enrolled in financial coa
knowledge and a recalibration
must have the tools to not re
As we're doing the work, I u
some untapped gifts inside of
work: credit repair, budgetin
developing the picture of Pu

rporated into their life now?
uity are required at the very
e community? This is the fog
ns.

know is we're not always in
neditate on an idea or set of
rried about the lights being
ly stewarding the money we
o operate on purpose in this

g to operate in Purpose, you
scribed as the transformation
d. Many, many of my clients
 with me, they are dreaming
 backroom is clean, they can

work in 2019. I attended a
d how important it is for the
in your shoe to travel in the
many times but this time it
the summit I had coached a
of service and ensuring that
or. We talked about products,
she needed to charge enough
es and reinvest in herself and

At hearing those words in
echoed in my mind. I heard my
words were lessons to me. I had a
thermostat. Before that summit,
was growing, I had SIGNIFIC
something big. I had so many an
around me as friends and suppor
really effect change in the world. I
series where I brought in Lisa Nic
coaches for finance, fitness, relati
teaching for 5 separate sessions.

While the goal was to char
wholeness in all these topics, I w
quit after every session, and not
Doing the series, I did not know
on an event of this magnitude an
did not have before the series. F
happened in my life and the lives
realized in that coaching session
did the series, my tongue in my m
not traveling in the same directic
said or was deceiving in any way,
that came as a result of the debt I
lives. It was time to recalibrate m

What I learned was that th
serve. It's not what you do, it's hc

ily find my way back to struggle,
arning lots of money. Even with
ves. Even with powerful friends.
millionaires. I was for the first

he floor, I did the work to change
. It's my birthright. I no longer
like a success. I wanted to serve
aselines for what I wanted my
to earn personally. Since making
gotten 100,000 very unexpected
stery, operating in purpose, and
journey. The sites along the way
yourself evolve. But not just you,
ndings. So it is a worthy journey.

C H

REAR-V

Often I sit and reflect. L
challenges I've had to overco
life would have been different
on in life. I have no regrets
Everything is perfect. But for
happened if I'd gotten on this

- • My children c upbringing

- • I would have in various stages of t existence I lived

- • I could have s just loving on my fam

- • I could have g develop their gifts ea music, dance, theatre

s earlier on which would have
sing the children to different
eir horizons

le enough to help my children

vely and possibly purchased
f the world before now

r since the cheapest foods are

ent properties earlier which

into my philanthropic side
struggle less

ed communities earlier and
es, and trajectories of many,
ified my Purpose and begun

have changed if things were
l list is much, MUCH longer.
of the work I've done for my
completed my programs, it lets
nancial liberation is necessary
ndemic, unemployment rates
, and businesses closing in
now. Everything is perfect.

You reading this now is perfect.
to master money at a time when
Your mastering money now will p
and your time to operate fully in
impact the world is now. Your pu
And you do not get to hold what

C H

ROADMA

My Purpose pays me ł
work as a Financial Wellness ؟
Purpose will pay you handsor
individuals, and husband aı
Accidental Entrepreneurs. M

1. Their immediate act
2. The moment they ic
3. When they earn tʰ
   created
4. When they achieve
   a result of our work

I have so many stories oı
clients because not only do we
up as negative items on their c
debt, and a lifestyle of pover
hindrances that further expla

and a slew of other avoidable
son is supplied the right tools
their money.

to repossession. Now because
her credit and because I had
making such a mistake before,
was illegal. I remember having
al dispute letter about the car.
ly did the lender change how
eports, they immediately sent
invested in that car, including
me, you know my thought
h over $10,000 that fast then
heard the news of her receipt
ed to the states, I sent a letter
illegal actions to which they
ry short time. Needless to say,
y and settle, to her advantage,
ng negative items in her file.
for her first home.

ouple that recently graduated
their forever home for their
e by a friend who is a real estate
y followed every instruction.
en they initially started, I was
not had the revelation about
cial psychological houses yet.

I became certified and structure
then I offered this service to them
away by countering my discoun
price as they were convinced tha
up to that point, had changed the
of their 2 beautiful children and
way I explained when they first s
to them seemed like the next log
full price for that.

Who knew that the person
would become a financial guide
to their path of Purpose and supp
free? Who knew that I would he
and access working capital as th
fire their bosses? Who knew the
the work that you love, being pr
for it, and having the freedom,
your dreams?

I wish I could stand here f
of a doubt that I knew. I suspec
fully evolved into what it is now
honestly say, I did not know. M
I took the time to sufficiently lea
I would turn around and teach
teach how to do the work it tak
would teach you how to re-estab

teach you how to remove your ... frequency. I would teach money ... ous resources on getting insanely ... I would teach how Purpose helps ... how to pass that wealth down to ... would in turn become the guide ...

... me was a short journey. People ... it repair. I gave them what they ... ry way. Now that journey begins ... ir and financial coaching, then ... ey mastery, and business credit, ... ancial coaching. Some people ... icial Wellness Strategist because ... pay bills but that's the extent of ... prove their financial acumen.

... ose unveils over time. As you ... plan becomes available to you. ... specialty in the area you want to ... at road can be bumpy and seem

... our superpower. It is the filter ... llows you to pivot and remain ... hange. It's the oil on your life. ... so the thing you can charge the ... y knack for making it look, feel,

taste, and sound like no one ... up you can innovate and ma... that will always enable you to ... innovation and entrepreneur... waters of competition and into ... Purpose is the reason you bre... else is gone and will be the spr... widow woman I previously in... natural gifting. It is the thing ... your first breath in this realm.

SECT

C H

I have a million "If on]
clients who have successfull
them identified their gifts late
impacting the world and the
serve. The best part is the free
Life.

1. You're not locked in

2. You're properly com

3. You get to determ
   schedule which fre
   with family and frie

4. The quality of you
   stress less and have

5. You tap into your a
   born to do.

his list, I urge you to get into our Purpose. You were not for a life of poverty. Life was he oppression of debt. I need n on purpose, for purpose, to

, David Burrus, "When you to multiplication. The Bible . You were called to multiply. 8x8 is 64. Time to multiply."

lenges that on a normal hike and a light snack. But on our sues, our limiting beliefs, our and anything else to distract not until we decide to offload ger serve us and keep us from uly get on our personal paths re we learned that everything at contributed to my success or things to become easy and n. We overcomplicate things in the first place.

're worth. But your purpose ou. As we all know, some xchange of your efforts for a

paycheck, someone is getting sha don't know you're being underpa are designed to pay you more. purpose is and who should bene an investor in your purpose wor is getting shafted because your h waiting for the day to fire him/o to know and be very clear that fulfillment and money because t than for a job you hate. This pos

I want financial abundance longer a part of your conversatio to another person and ask, "You t us to breathe tomorrow?" No or is air in abundance. I need you t Get out of that scarcity mindset a to go around and sustain us for change to this new filter, you wi more. You can earn it, use it, ir money is here for you in abunda

SEC

CHAP

HOW TO MAK
ONTO THE AVE

I want to give you a few pr
to redesign your financial life ex
are committed to this process, in
slow but as you progress, and yo
feel like so much of a chore.

1. Know your numbers!
   medical professional t
   this is your Financial
   your financial number
   I don't mean the Vanta
   Go to MyFICO.com. (
   have one and begin to f
   credit standing. Kno
   of 3 reports summariz
   report and understand
   begin to identify why

oing right. If your scores are not
lent across the board, Umbrella
expensive Do-It-Yourself Credit
epth teachings on how to dispute
ess and we even offer a bonus of
t just in case that does not come

s not stop at your scores. Do you
Do you pay all of your household
es it take to run your household
rself? Is your family financially
emergency or a natural disaster?
h you make and how much you
u are leaking money? How easy
se holes? Do you have 3, 6, or
onthly expenses saved in case of

arts of knowing your numbers is
ell versed in where you keep your
nce company contact numbers.
uate your home, are your most
s, insurance policies, warranties,
an be grabbed quickly and easily
must be left behind, are they in

2. Begin to document y
got that information
Do these beliefs sup

3. As you're looking
money if you have ch
you find yourself sa
children, what is a c
your friends? Are th
life experience you'r

4. When is the last ti
retirement accounts
If so, are they on pa
desired age? Do you

The bottom line is that
endeavors, you need someon
professional athletes did not
best coaches teaching them da
These coaches walk alongside
is no different with you and
financial coach or in my case,
your needs you have to be firs

1. What are your core
want to modify, cha

2. What is your Money

ınd make sure that the person
nce in helping clients achieve

1ot to eliminate your money
·eceive divine instructions on
may not be your coach. Our
?urpose helps you clean your
vou new financial skills, and
oney available to you. If this
sure there are other financial
prepared to help you.

·d end but be flexible enough

Financial, Inc., they are sure
ually, it's not until they arrive
 negative items on their credit
ire problem. Then when they
y get on the journey. I need
he part that always surprises
I say it will in the beginning.
1 how they can be monetized.

enough to find your personal
you into action with the steps
f anywhere in my story, then
ry out for all to see, worth it.
in Purpose and let that be a
ions.

Blessings.

If you want to learn more, I'ı
You can call today or visit my v
consultation-- a friendly, no-pr
Financial can help you master mc

Umbrella Financial, Inc

www.getufs.com

(866) 837-4103

CPSIA information can be obtained
at www.ICGtesting.com
Printed in the USA
LVHW081951200422
716460LV00047B/103